CHRISTMAS SONGS

50 Short Late Elementary Piano Solos with Optional Duet Accompaniments

Arranged by Tom Gerou

All titles in this book are proven to be time-tested Christmas favorites that can be enjoyed by both kids and adults. Care has been given to help make the music easy to play. These short, two-page selections are arranged in traditional five-finger style, with the melody split between the hands and without key signatures in the solo part. Dotted quarter notes, triplets, and sixteenth notes have been avoided. When there are lyrics, leader lines are also omitted to maintain an uncluttered look. All melodic arrangements have optional duet accompaniments for the fullest sound and maximum playing fun!

Produced by
Alfred Music
P.O. Box 10003
Van Nuys, CA 91410-0003
alfred.com

Printed in USA.

ISBN-10: 0-7390-9553-6
ISBN-13: 978-0-7390-9553-9

Contents

All I Want for Christmas Is My Two Front Teeth

Words and Music by Don Gardner
Arr. by Tom Gerou

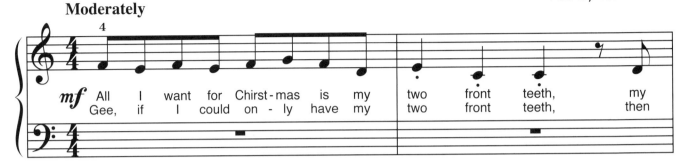

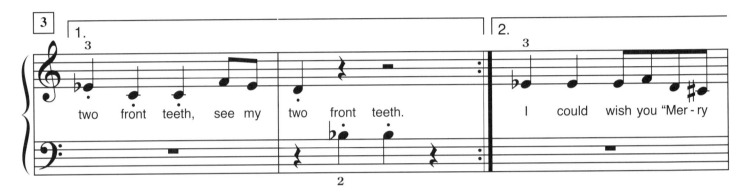

Optional Duet Accompaniment (Play solo part 1 octave higher than written.)

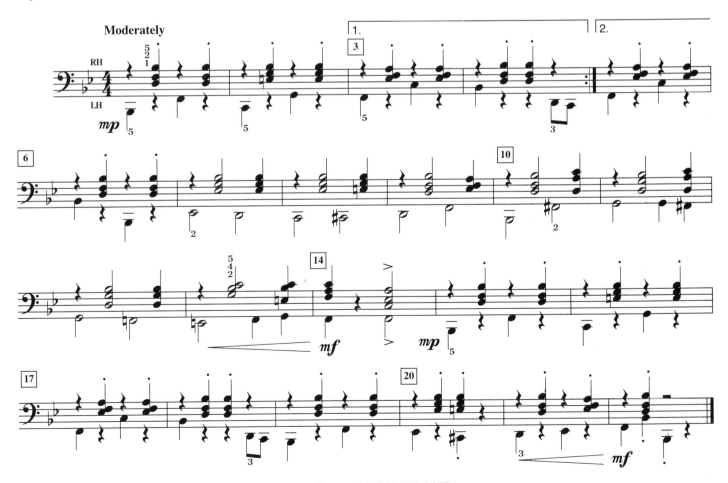

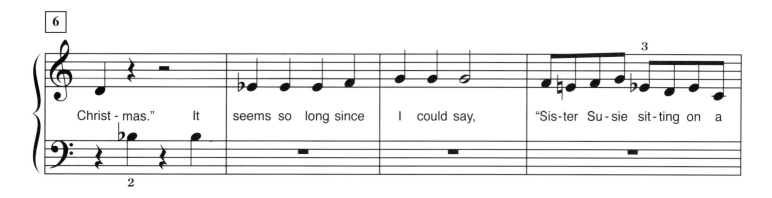

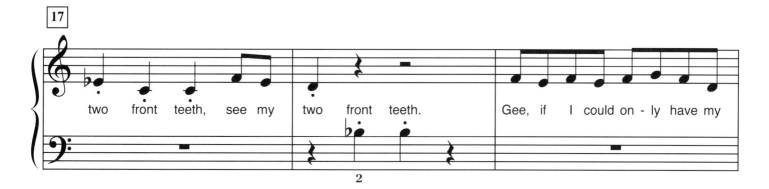
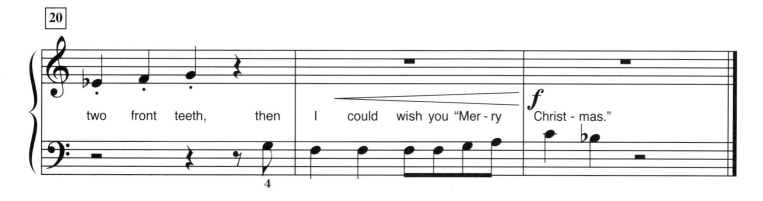

Angels We Have Heard on High

Traditional French Carol

Arr. by Tom Gerou

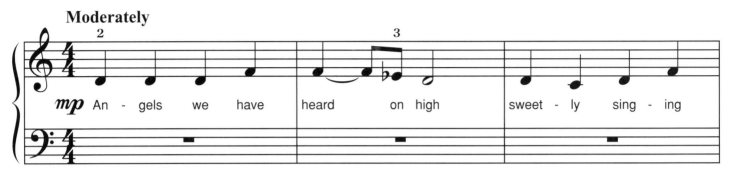

Optional Duet Accompaniment (Play solo part 1 octave higher than written.)

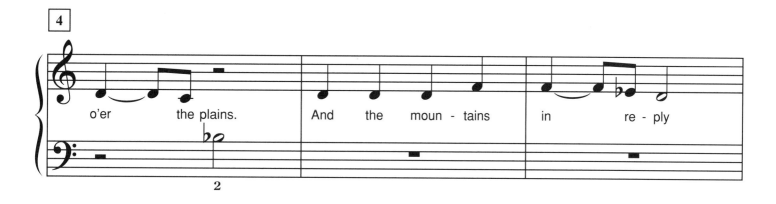

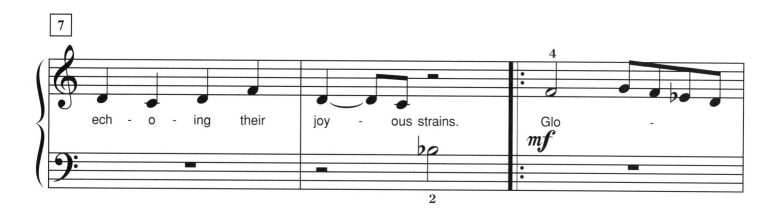

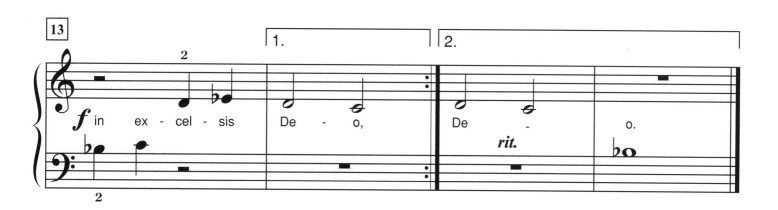

Arabian Dance
(from *The Nutcracker*)

Peter Ilyich Tchaikovsky
Arr. by Tom Gerou

Optional Duet Accompaniment (Play solo part 1 octave higher than written.)

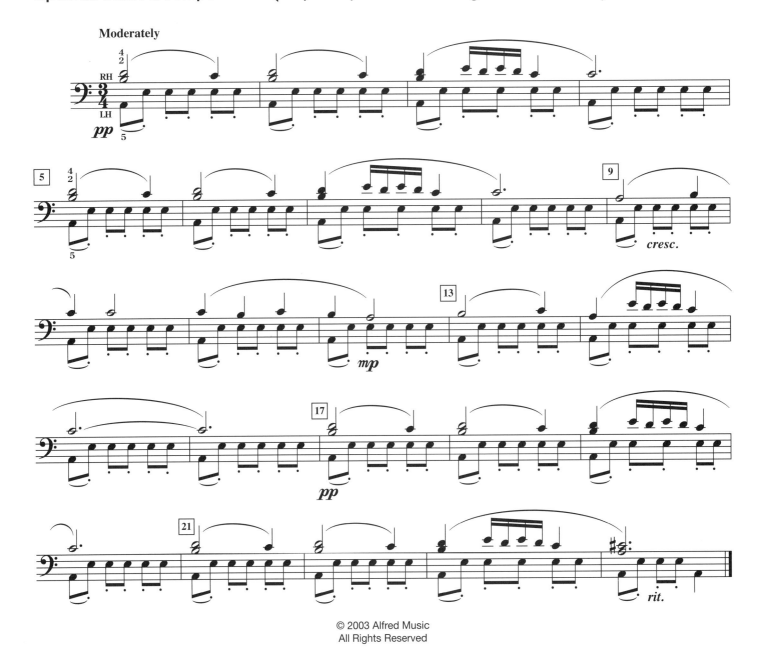

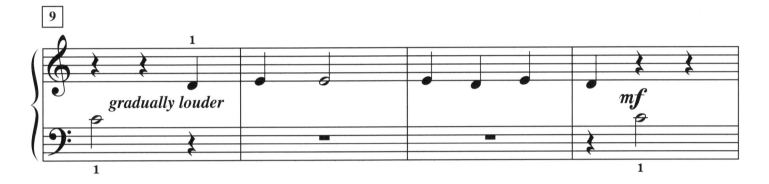

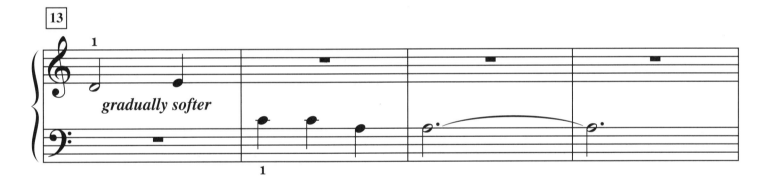

Away in a Manger

Music by James R. Murray

Arr. by Tom Gerou

Optional Duet Accompaniment (Play solo part 1 octave higher than written.)

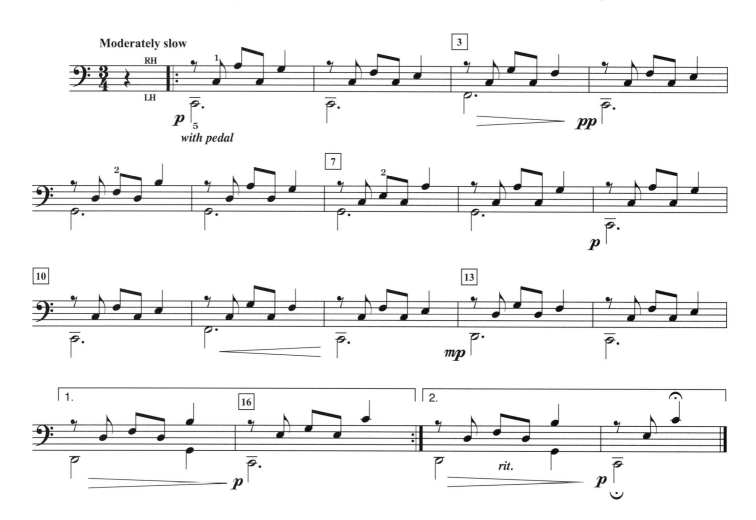

Believe
(from *The Polar Express*)

Words and Music by
Glen Ballard and Alan Silvestri
Arr. by Tom Gerou

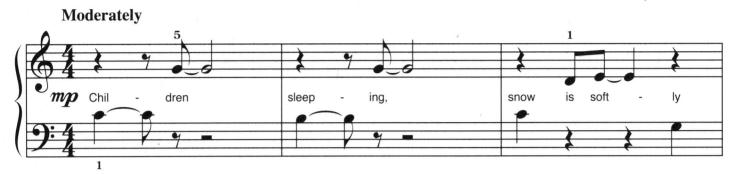

Optional Duet Accompaniment (Play solo part 1 octave higher than written.)

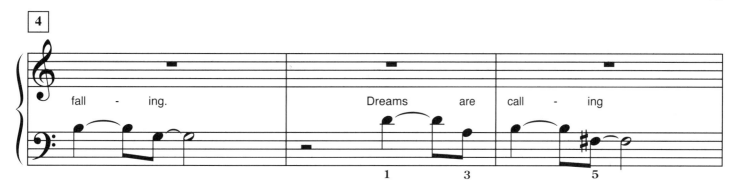

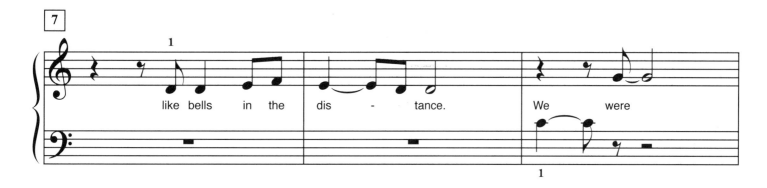

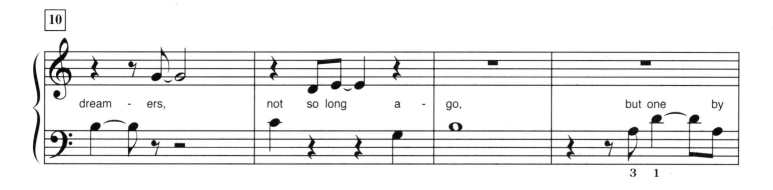

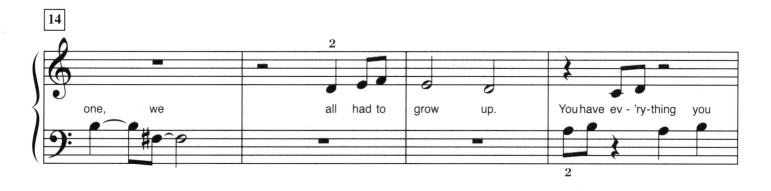

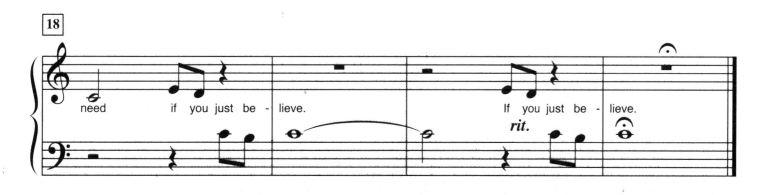

Chinese Dance
(from *The Nutcracker*)

Peter Ilyich Tchaikovsky

Arr. by Tom Gerou

Optional Duet Accompaniment (Play solo part 1 octave higher than written.)

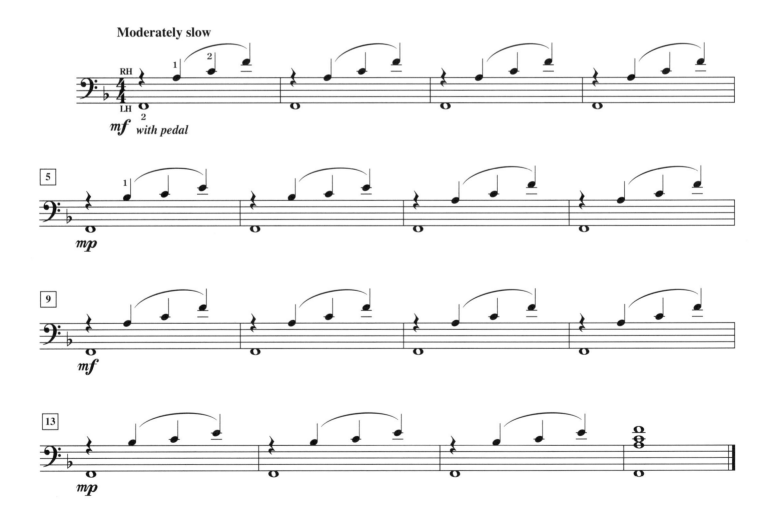

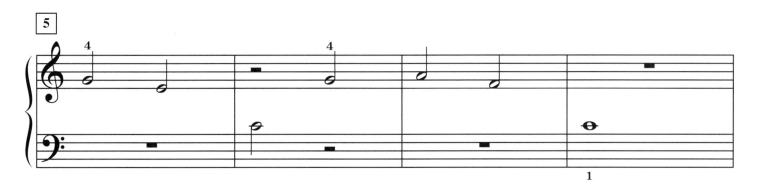

The Christmas Waltz

Words by Sammy Cahn
Music by Jule Styne

Arr. by Tom Gerou

Bright waltz tempo

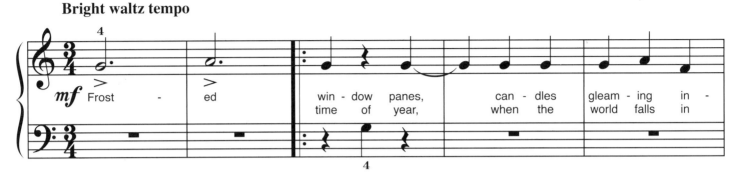

Optional Duet Accompaniment (Play solo part 1 octave higher than written.)

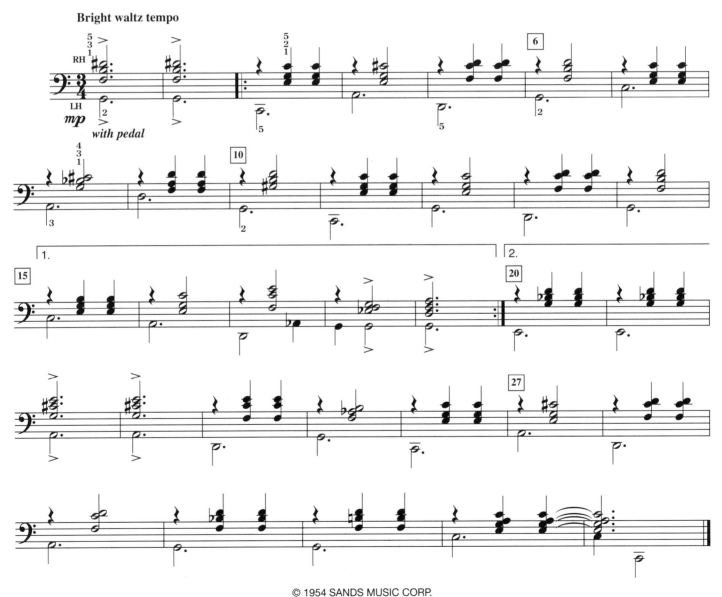

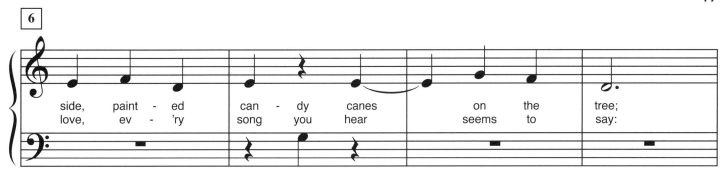

side, paint - ed can - dy canes on the tree;
love, ev - 'ry song you hear seems to say:

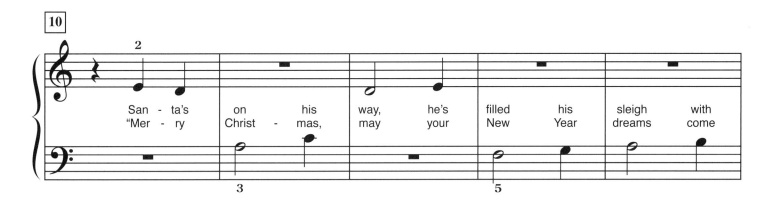

San - ta's on his way, he's filled his sleigh with
"Mer - ry Christ - mas, may your New Year dreams come

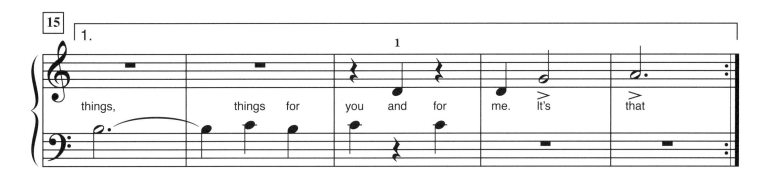

1.

things, things for you and for me. It's that

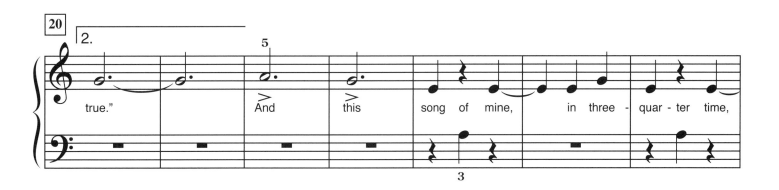

2.

true." And this song of mine, in three - quar - ter time,

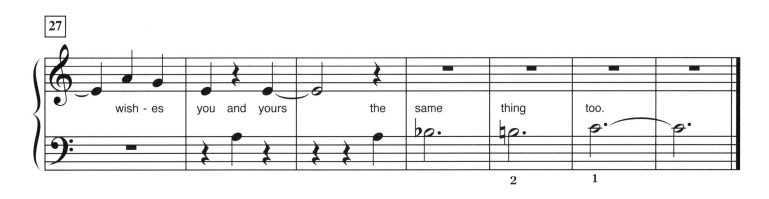

wish - es you and yours the same thing too.

Dance of the Reed Flutes
(from *The Nutcracker*)

Peter Ilyich Tchaikovsky
Arr. by Tom Gerou

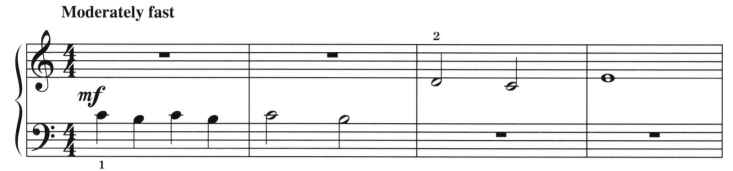

Optional Duet Accompaniment (Play solo part 1 octave higher than written.)

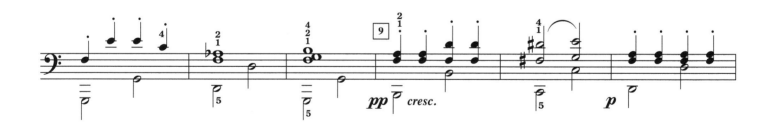

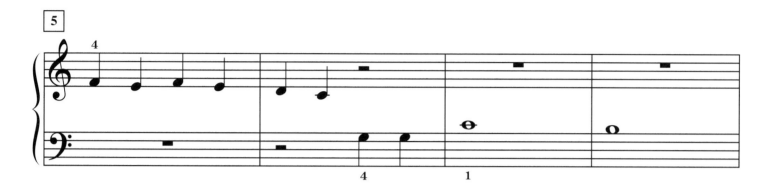

Dance of the Sugar Plum Fairy
(from *The Nutcracker*)

Peter Ilyich Tchaikovsky

Arr. by Tom Gerou

Optional Duet Accompaniment (Play solo part 1 octave higher than written.)

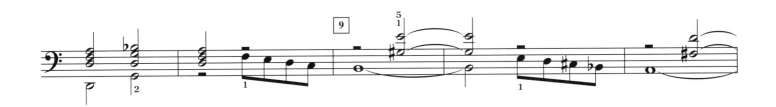

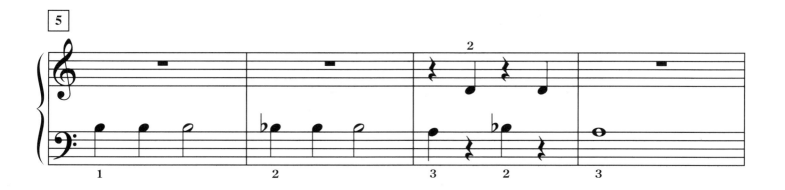

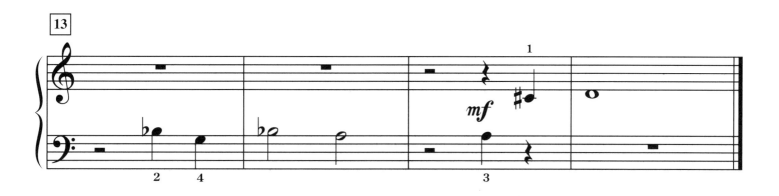

Deck the Halls

Traditional
Arr. by Tom Gerou

Moderately fast

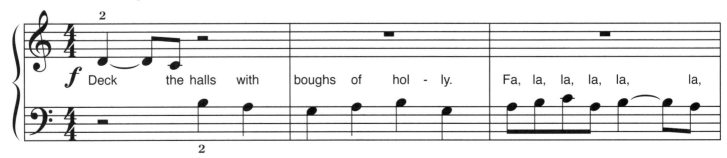

Deck the halls with boughs of hol - ly. Fa, la, la, la, la, la,

Optional Duet Accompaniment (Play solo part 1 octave higher than written.)

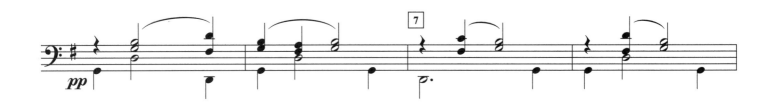

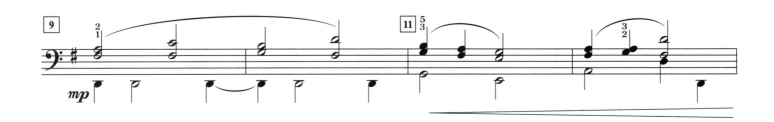

Felíz Navidad

Words and Music by José Feliciano
Arr. by Tom Gerou

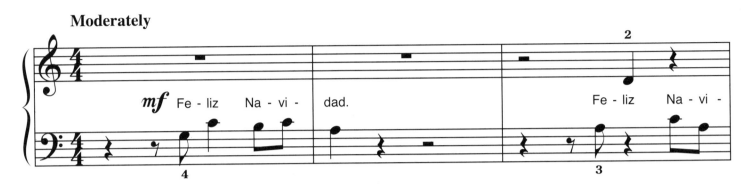

Optional Duet Accompaniment (Play solo part 1 octave higher than written.)

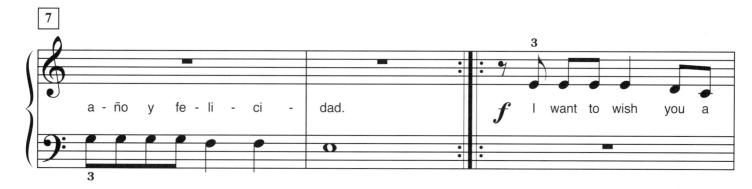

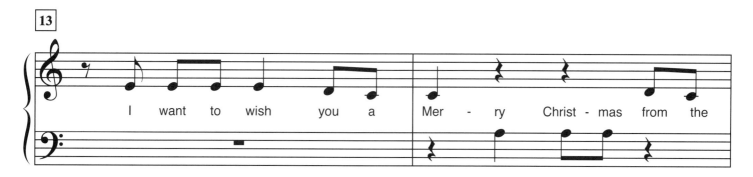

The First Noel

Traditional
Arr. by Tom Gerou

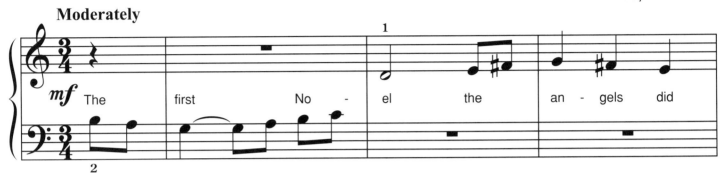

Optional Duet Accompaniment (Play solo part 1 octave higher than written.)

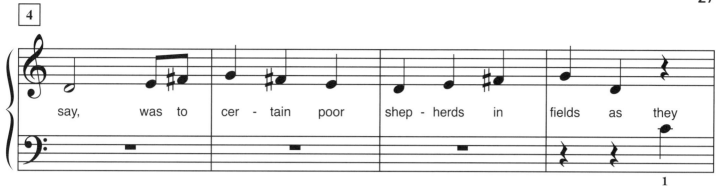

say, was to cer - tain poor shep - herds in fields as they

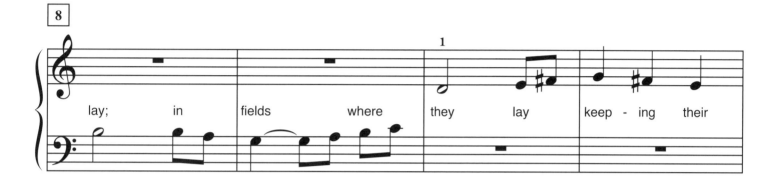

lay; in fields where they lay keep - ing their

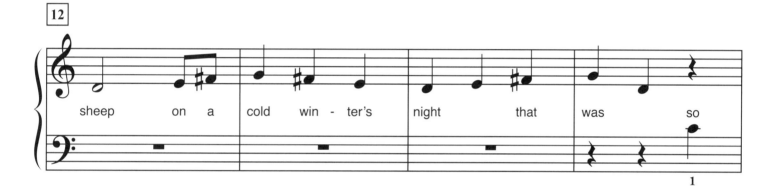

sheep on a cold win - ter's night that was so

deep. *f* No - el, No - el, No - el, No -

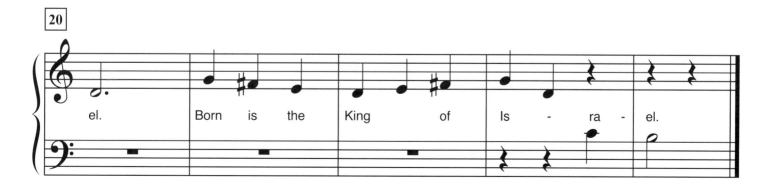

el. Born is the King of Is - ra - el.

Frosty the Snowman

Words and Music by
Steve Nelson and Jack Rollins

Arr. by Tom Gerou

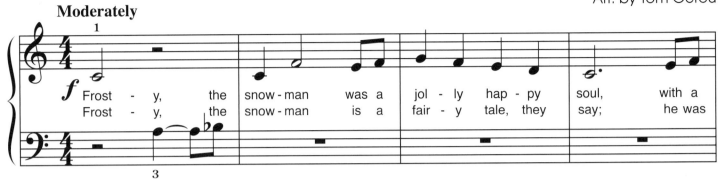

Optional Duet Accompaniment (Play solo part 1 octave higher than written.)

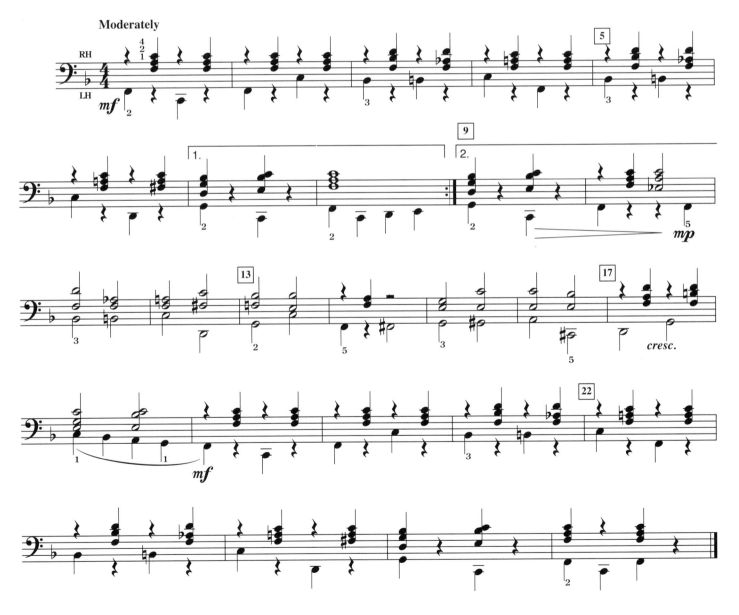

29

God Rest Ye Merry, Gentlemen

Traditional
Arr. by Tom Gerou

Moderately slow

Lyrics: God rest ye mer - ry, gen - tle - men, let

Optional Duet Accompaniment (Play solo part 1 octave higher than written.)

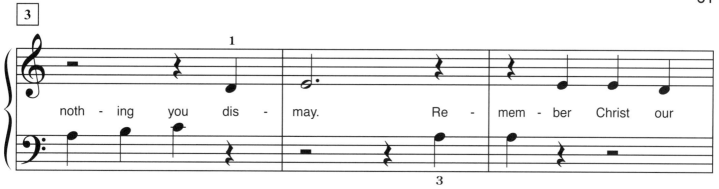

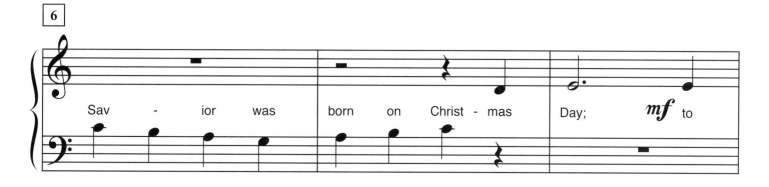

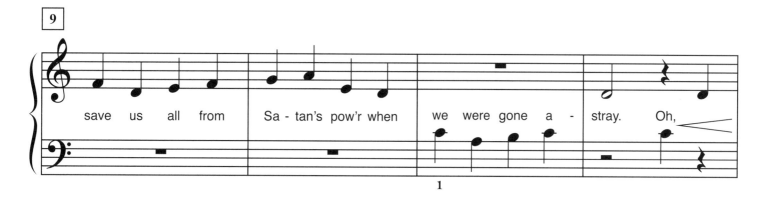

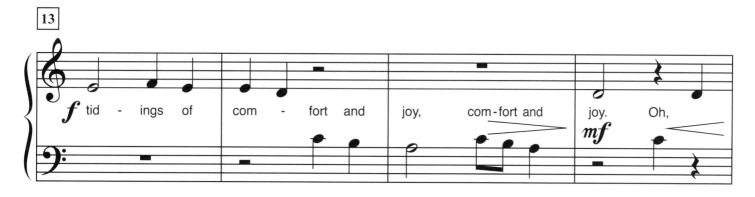

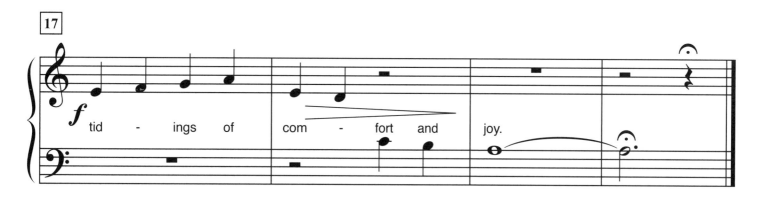

Good King Wenceslas

Traditional
Words by John Mason Neale
Arr. by Tom Gerou

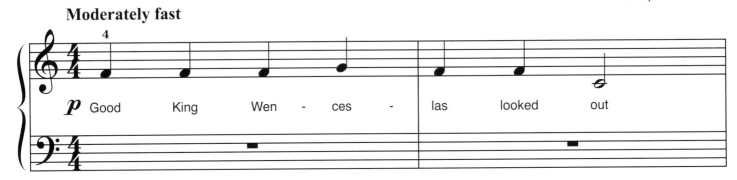

Optional Duet Accompaniment (Play solo part 1 octave higher than written.)

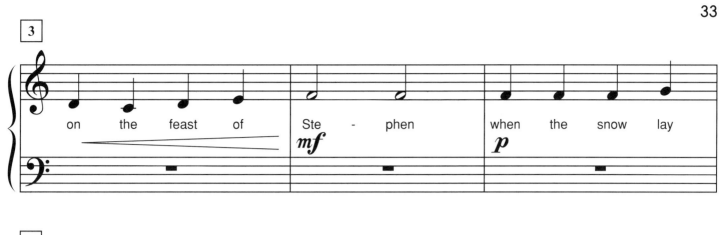

on the feast of Ste - phen when the snow lay

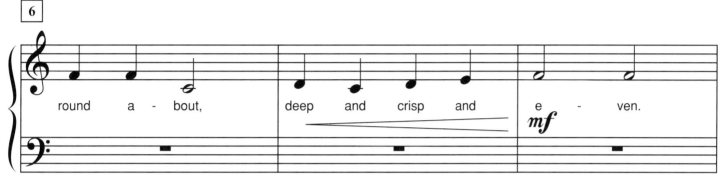

round a - bout, deep and crisp and e - ven.

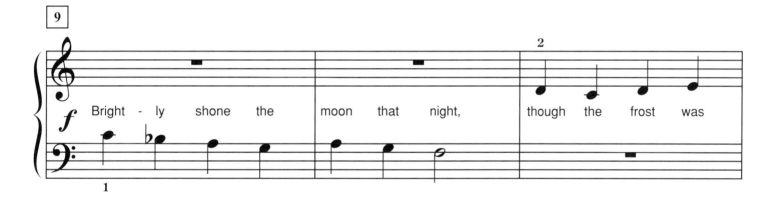

Bright - ly shone the moon that night, though the frost was

cru - el, when a poor man came in sight

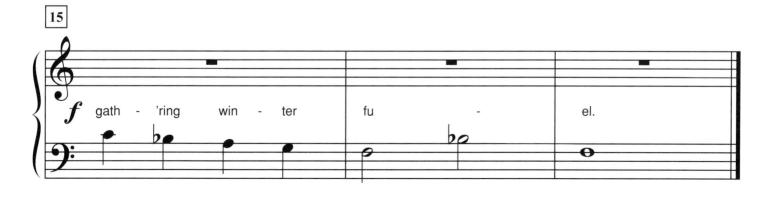

gath - 'ring win - ter fu - el.

Hark! The Herald Angels Sing

Words by Charles Wesley
Music by Felix Mendelssohn

Arr. by Tom Gerou

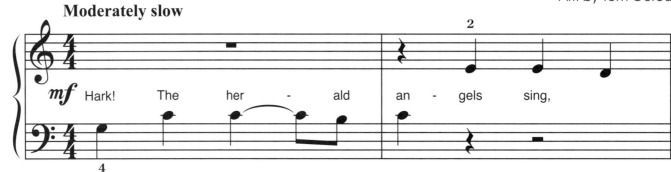

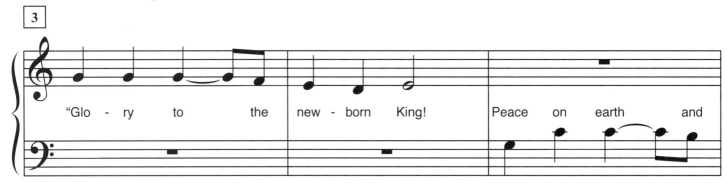

Optional Duet Accompaniment (Play solo part 1 octave higher than written.)

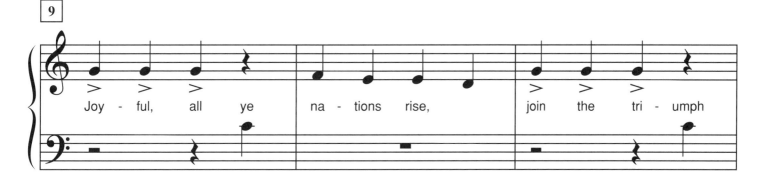

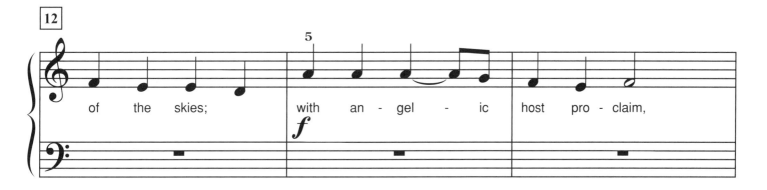

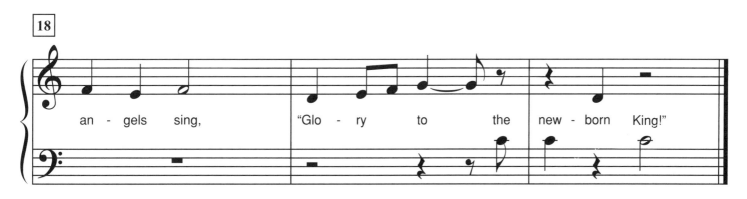

Have Yourself a Merry Little Christmas

Words and Music by
Hugh Martin and Ralph Blane

Arr. by Tom Gerou

Optional Duet Accompaniment (Play solo part 1 octave higher than written.)

From now on, our troub-les will be out of sight.

Through the years we all will be to-geth-er, if the fates al - low.

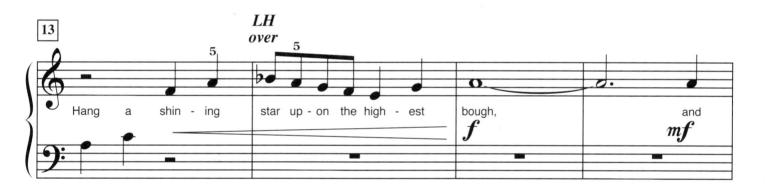

Hang a shin - ing star up-on the high - est bough, and

have your-self a mer-ry lit-tle Christ-mas now.

A Holly Jolly Christmas

Words and Music by Johnny Marks
Arr. by Tom Gerou

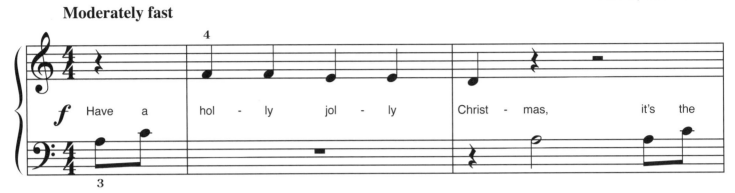

Optional Duet Accompaniment (Play solo part 1 octave higher than written.)

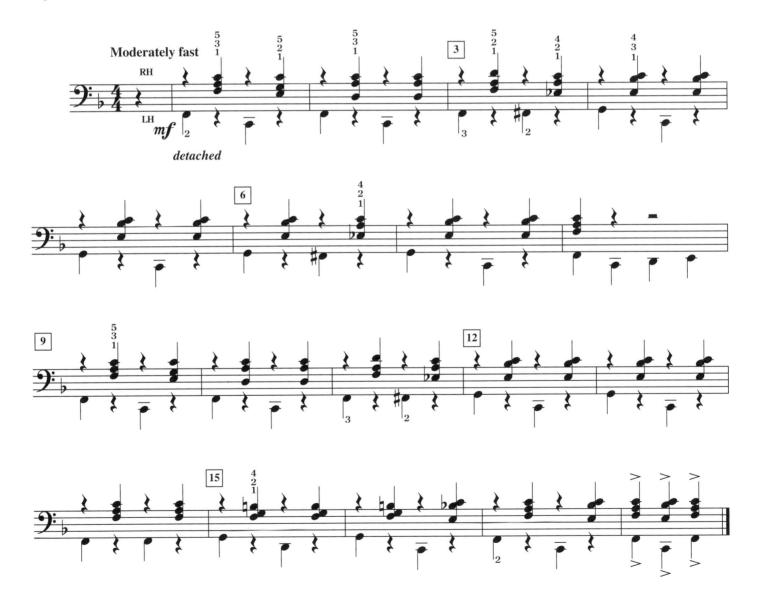

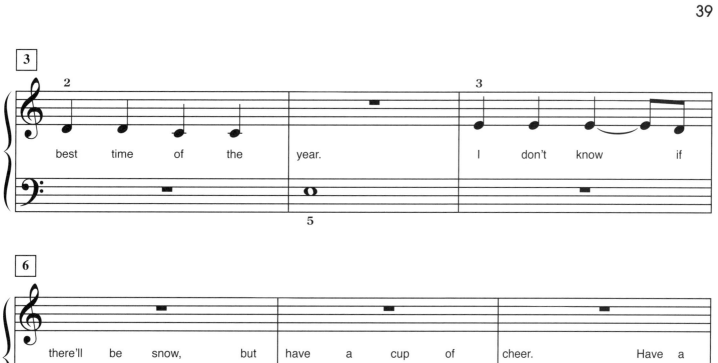

best time of the year. I don't know if

there'll be snow, but have a cup of cheer. Have a

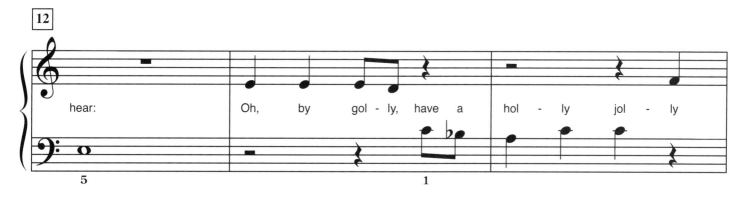

hol - ly jol - ly Christ - mas, and in case you did - n't

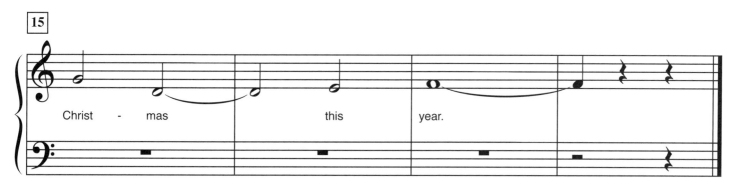

hear: Oh, by gol - ly, have a hol - ly jol - ly

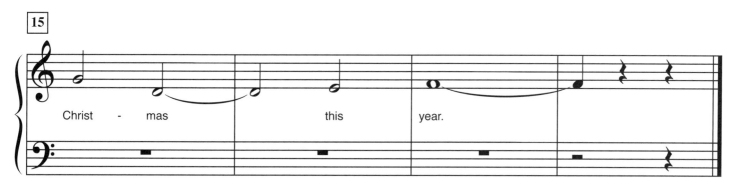

Christ - mas this year.

(There's No Place Like)
Home for the Holidays

Words by Al Stillman
Music by Robert Allen

Arr. by Tom Gerou

Moderately slow

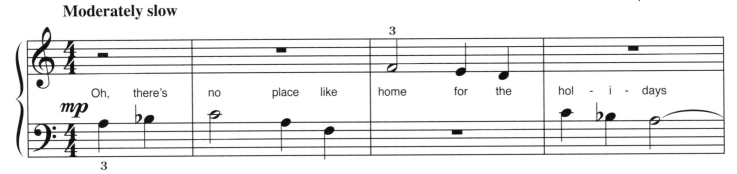

Oh, there's no place like home for the hol - i - days

Optional Duet Accompaniment (Play solo part 1 octave higher than written.)

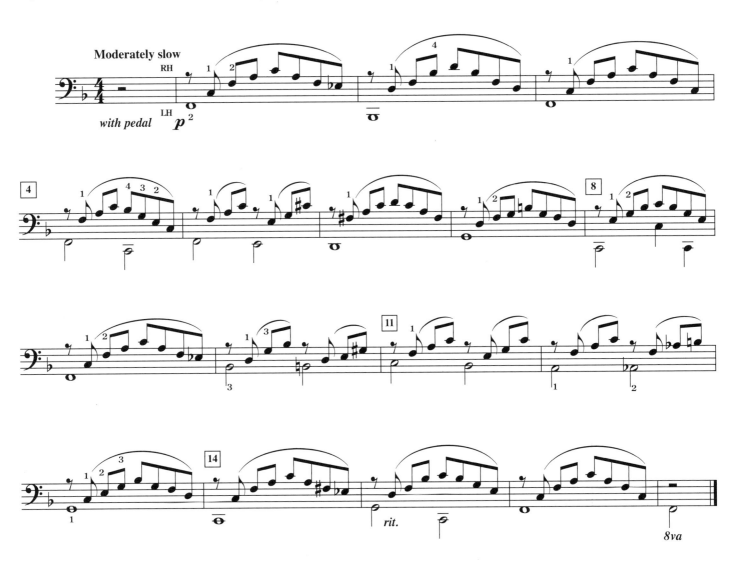

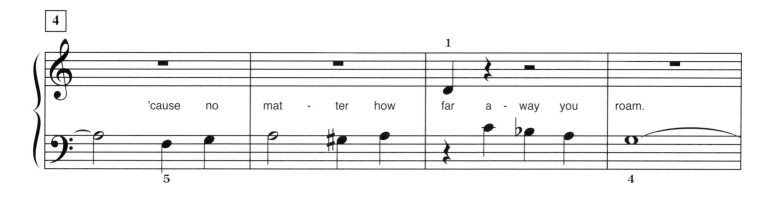

'cause no mat - ter how far a - way you roam.

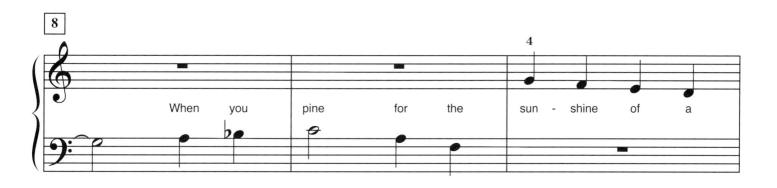

When you pine for the sun - shine of a

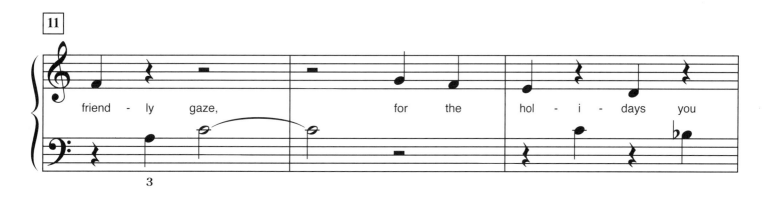

friend - ly gaze, for the hol - i - days you

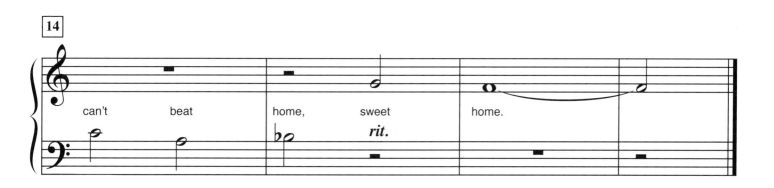

can't beat home, sweet home.

rit.

I Saw Three Ships

Traditional English Carol
Arr. by Tom Gerou

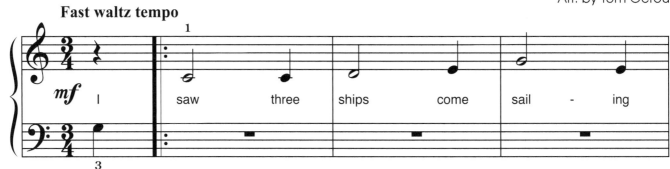

Optional Duet Accompaniment (Play solo part 1 octave higher than written.)

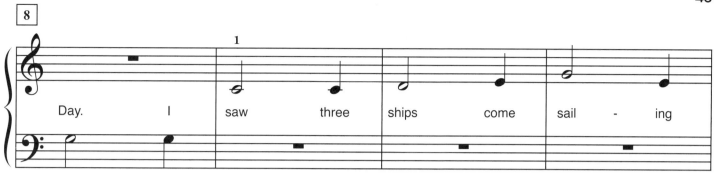

Day. I saw three ships come sail - ing

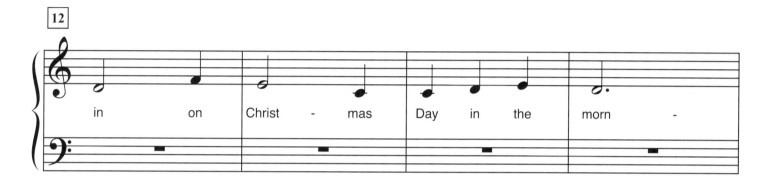

in on Christ - mas Day in the morn -

ing. *f* *mf*

1.–8. 9.

f *mf* And

2. And what was in those ships all three,
   On Christmas Day, on Christmas Day?
   And what was in those ships all three,
   On Christmas Day in the morning?

3. Our Savior Christ and His Lady,
   On Christmas Day, on Christmas Day?
   And what was in those ships all three,
   On Christmas Day in the morning?

4. Pray, whither sailed those ships all three?…

5. O, they sailed into Bethlehem…

6. And all the bells on earth shall ring…

7. And all the angels in Heav'n shall sing…

8. And all the souls on earth shall sing…

9. Then let us all rejoice again…

I'll Be Home for Christmas

Words by Kim Gannon
Music by Walter Kent

Arr. by Tom Gerou

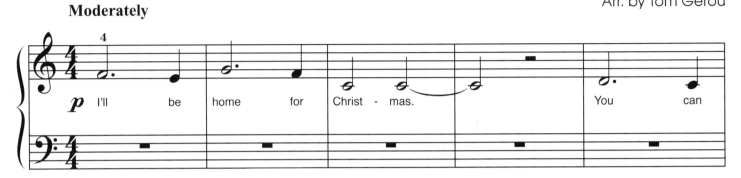

I'll be home for Christ - mas. You can

Optional Duet Accompaniment (Play solo part 1 octave higher than written.)

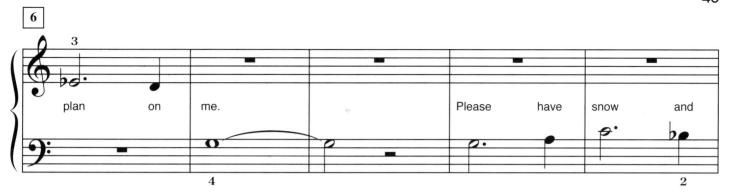

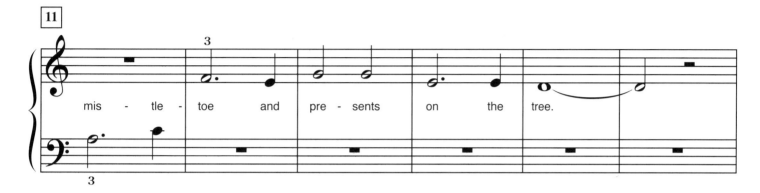

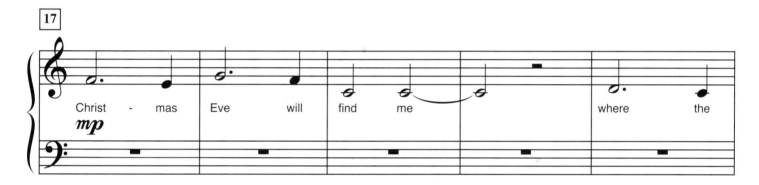

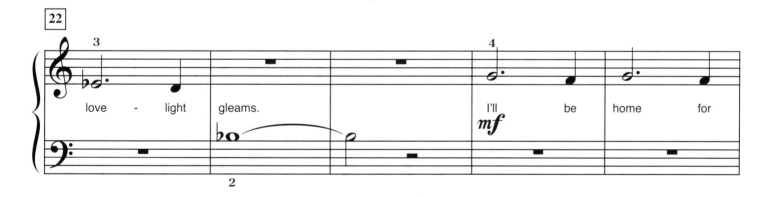

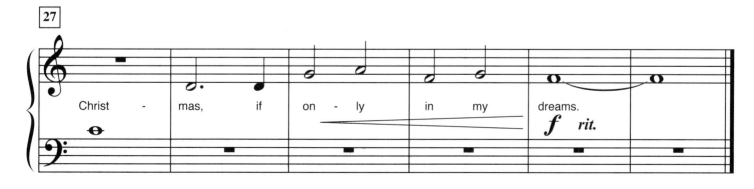

It Came upon the Midnight Clear

Words by Edmund H. Sears
Music by Richard Storrs Willis
Arr. by Tom Gerou

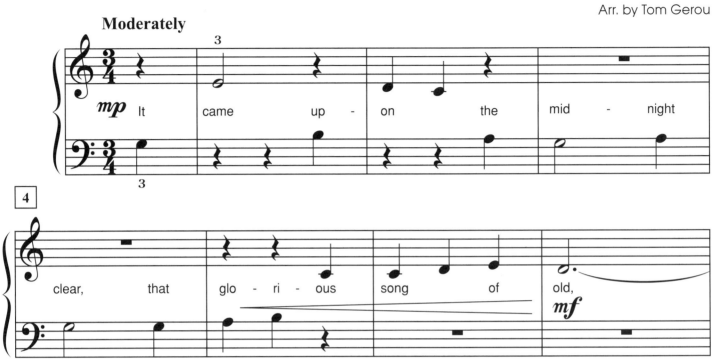

Optional Duet Accompaniment (Play solo part 1 octave higher than written.)

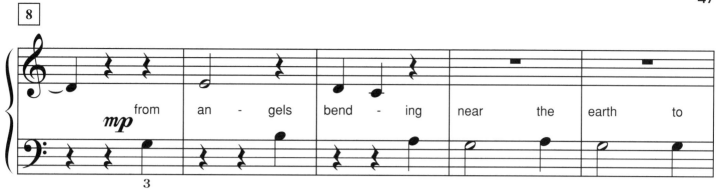

from an - gels bend - ing near the earth to

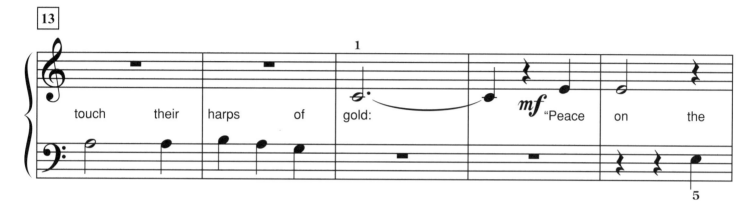

touch their harps of gold: "Peace on the

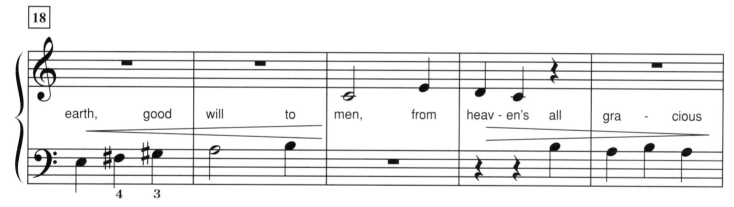

earth, good will to men, from heav - en's all gra - cious

King!" The world in sol - emn

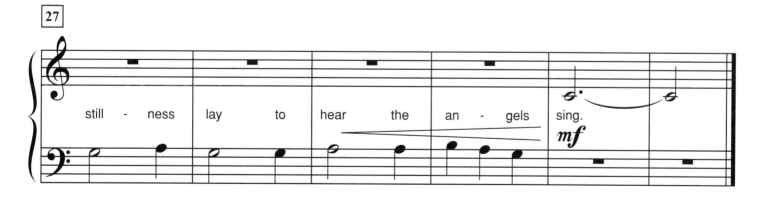

still - ness lay to hear the an - gels sing.

It's the Most Wonderful Time of the Year

Words and Music by
Eddie Pola and George Wyle

Arr. by Tom Gerou

Bright waltz tempo

Optional Duet Accompaniment (Play solo part 1 octave higher than written.)

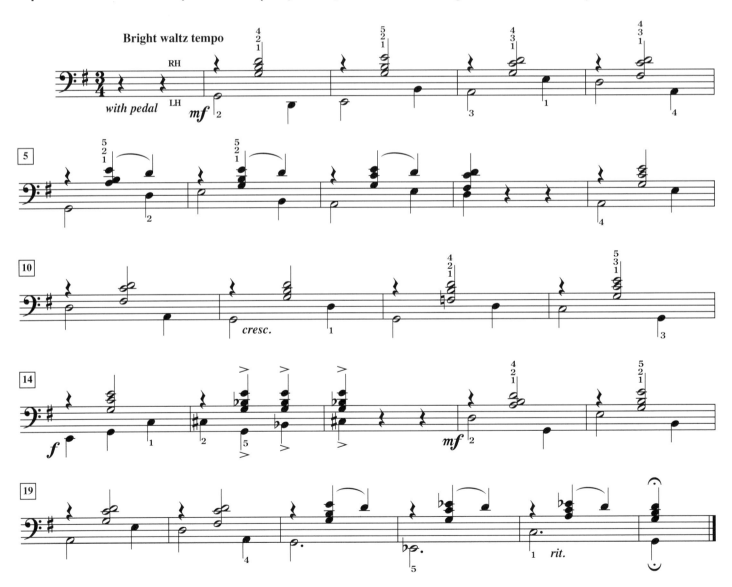

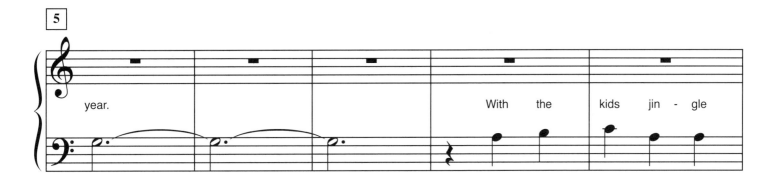

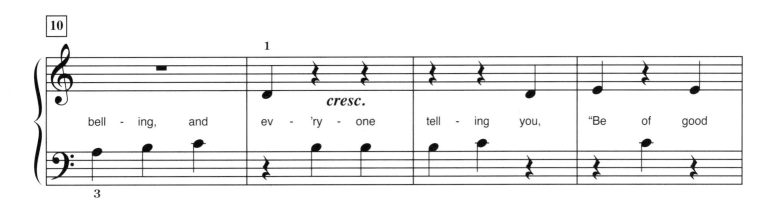

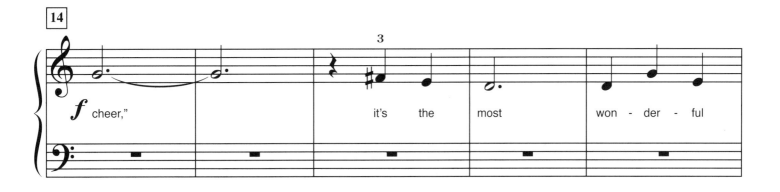

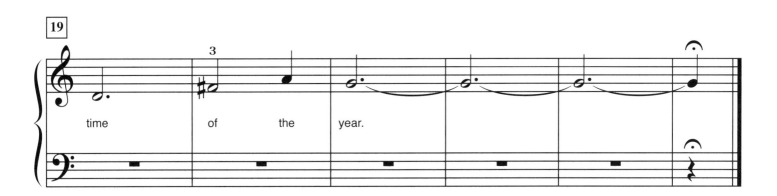

Jingle Bell Rock

Words and Music by Joe Beal and Jim Boothe
Arr. by Tom Gerou

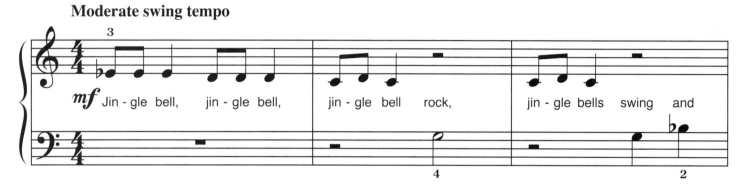

Moderate swing tempo

Jin - gle bell, jin - gle bell, jin - gle bell rock, jin - gle bells swing and

Optional Duet Accompaniment (Play solo part 1 octave higher than written.)

Jingle Bells

Words and Music by James Pierpont
Arr. by Tom Gerou

Optional Duet Accompaniment (Play solo part 1 octave higher than written.)

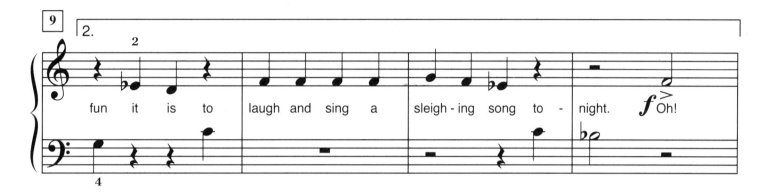

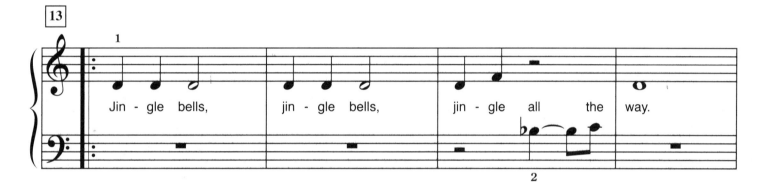

Jolly Old Saint Nicholas

Traditional
Arr. by Tom Gerou

Optional Duet Accompaniment (Play solo part 1 octave higher than written.)

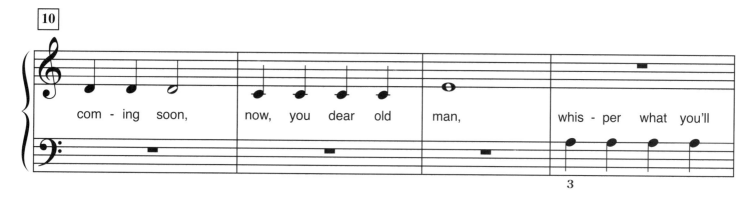

10 com - ing soon, | now, you dear old | man, | whis - per what you'll

14 bring to me, | tell me if you | can. *p* When the clock is | strik - ing twelve,

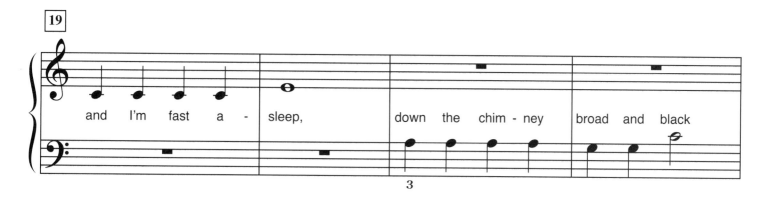

19 and I'm fast a - | sleep, | down the chim - ney | broad and black

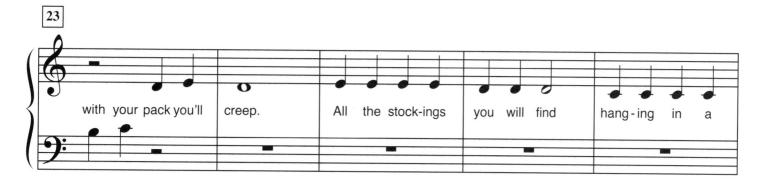

23 with your pack you'll | creep. | All the stock-ings | you will find | hang - ing in a

28 row, | mine will be the | short - est one, | you'll be sure to | know.

Joy to the World

Words by Isaac Watts
Music by Lowell Mason

Arr. by Tom Gerou

Optional Duet Accompaniment (Play solo part 1 octave higher than written.)

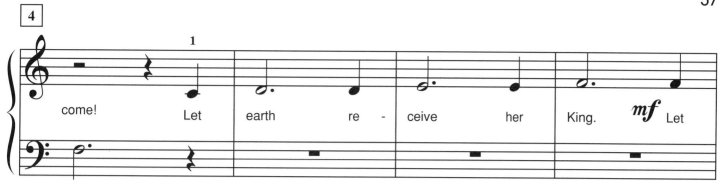

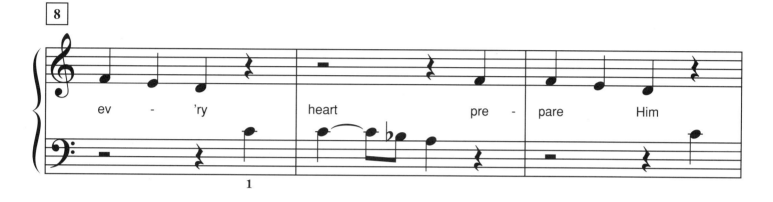

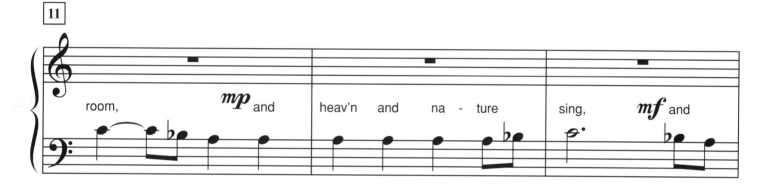

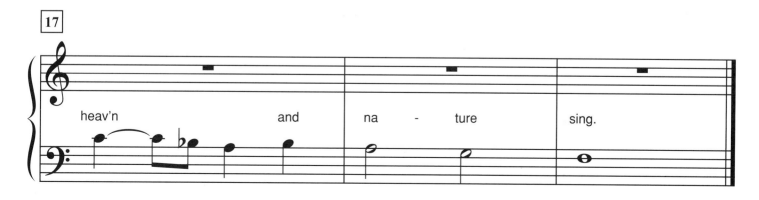

Let It Snow! Let It Snow! Let It Snow!

Words by Sammy Cahn
Music by Jule Styne

Arr. by Tom Gerou

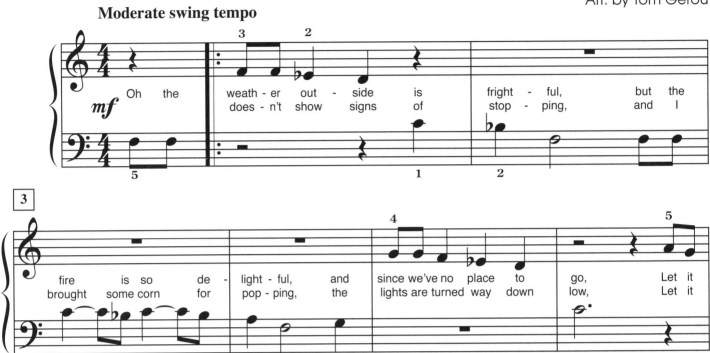

Optional Duet Accompaniment (Play solo part 1 octave higher than written.)

snow! Let it snow! Let it snow! It snow! When we
snow! Let it snow! Let it

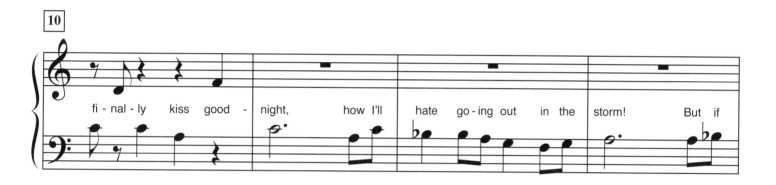

fi - nal - ly kiss good - night, how I'll hate go - ing out in the storm! But if

you'll real - ly hold me tight, all the way home I'll be warm. The

fire is slow - ly dy - ing, and, my dear, we're still good - bye - ing, but as

long as you love me so, Let it snow! Let it snow! Let it snow!

The Little Drummer Boy

Words and Music by Katherine Davis,
Henry Onorati, and Harry Simeone
Arr. by Tom Gerou

Optional Duet Accompaniment (Play solo part 1 octave higher than written.)

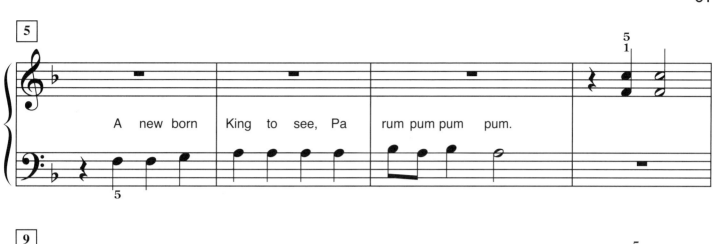

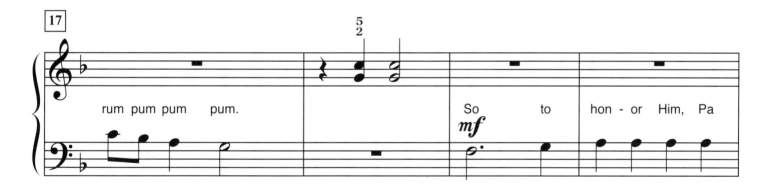

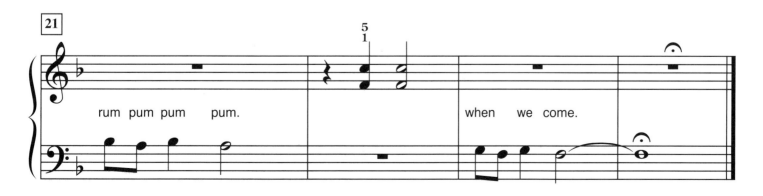

A Marshmallow World

Words by Carl Sigman
Music by Peter De Rose

Arr. by Tom Gerou

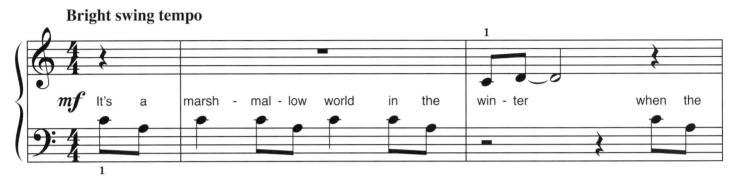

Optional Duet Accompaniment (Play solo part 1 octave higher than written.)

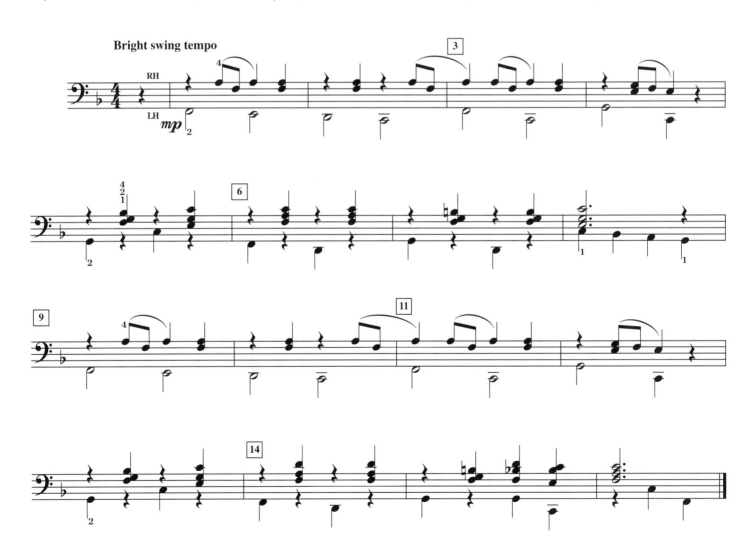

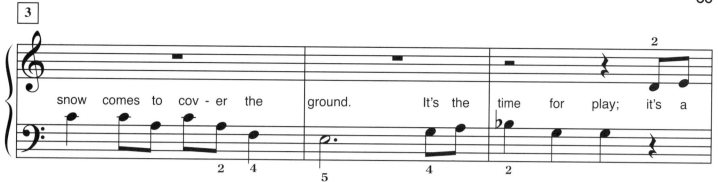

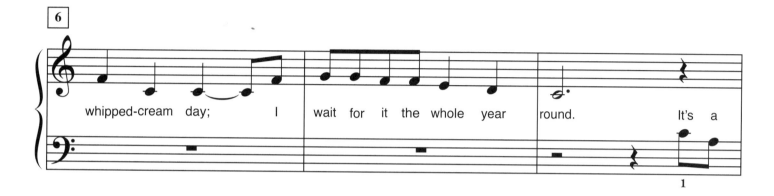

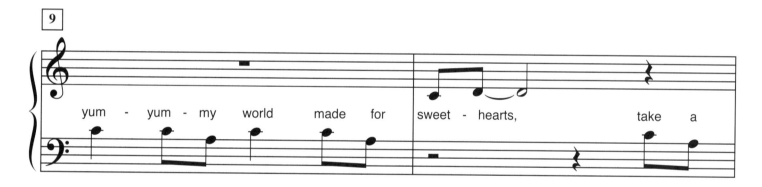

O Christmas Tree

Traditional
Arr. by Tom Gerou

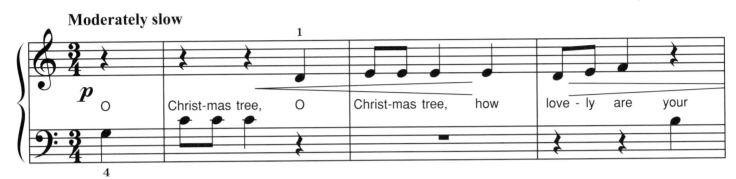

Optional Duet Accompaniment (Play solo part 1 octave higher than written.)

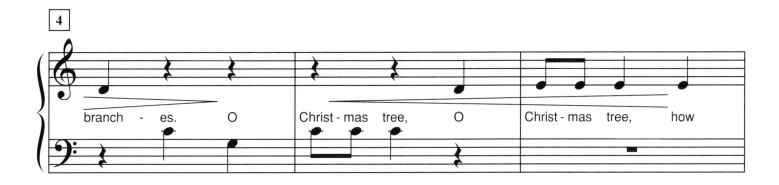

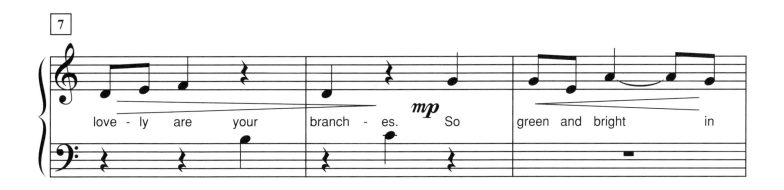

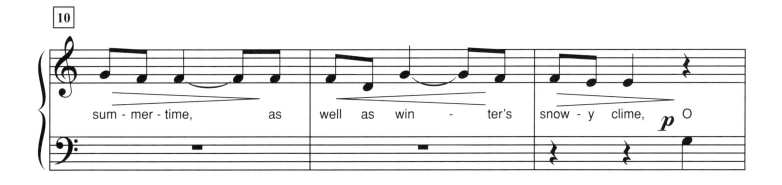

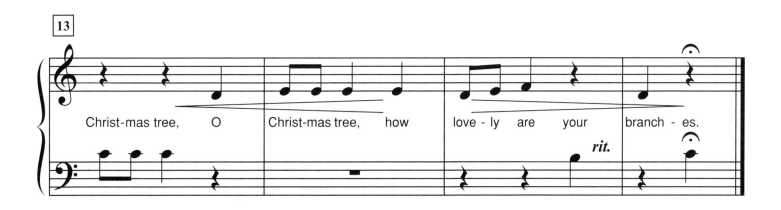

O Come, All Ye Faithful

John Francis Wade

Arr. by Tom Gerou

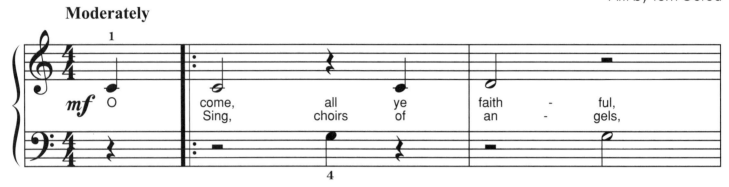

Optional Duet Accompaniment (Play solo part 1 octave higher than written.)

67

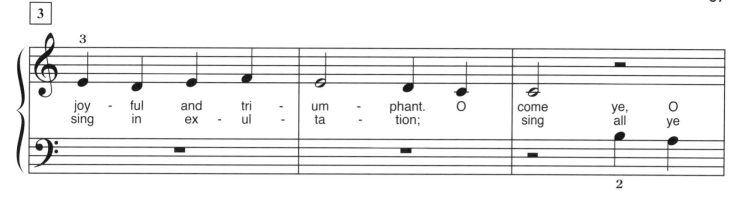

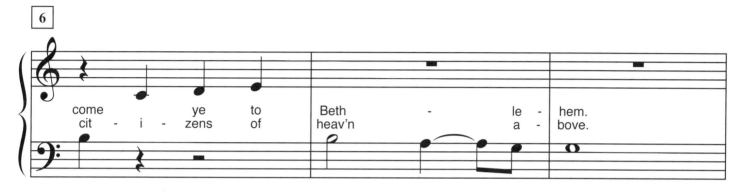

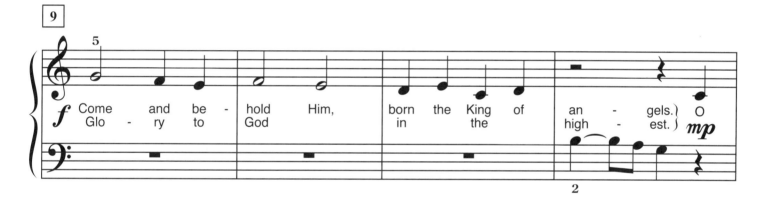

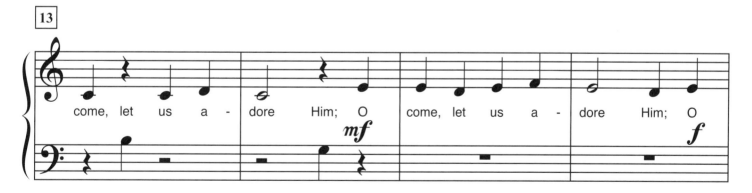

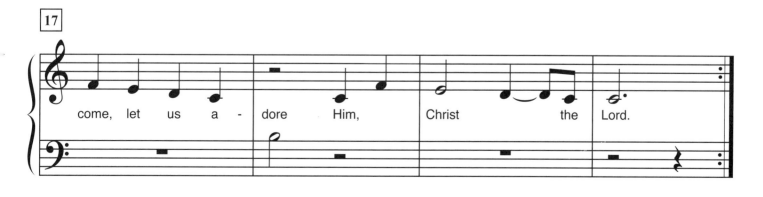

O Little Town of Bethlehem

Words by Phillips Brooks
Music by Lewis H. Redner
Arr. by Tom Gerou

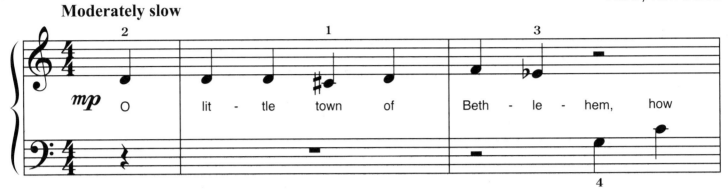

Optional Duet Accompaniment (Play solo part 1 octave higher than written.)

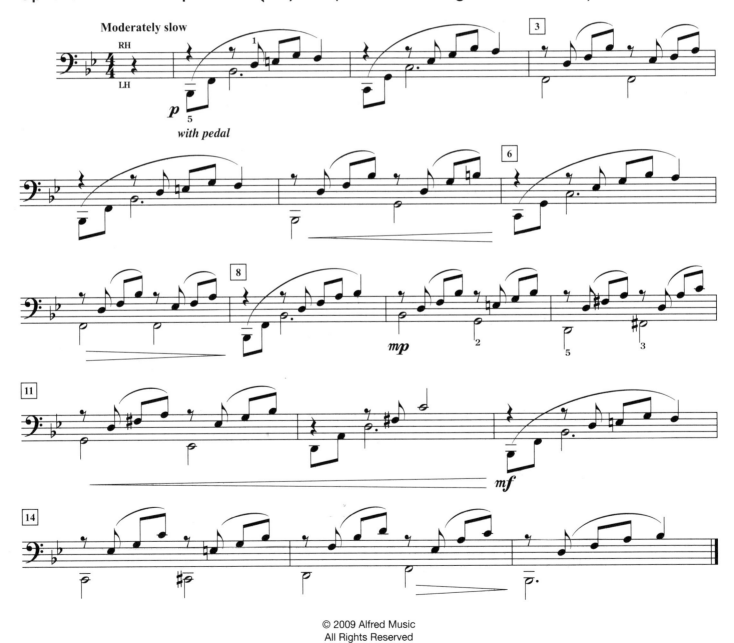

Overture
(from *The Nutcracker*)

Peter Ilyich Tchaikovsky

Arr. by Tom Gerou

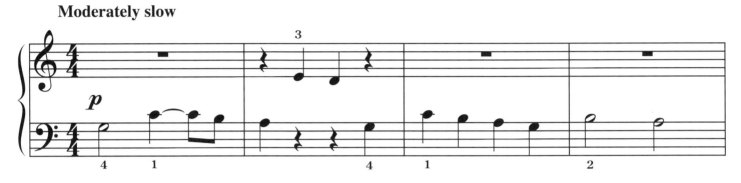

Optional Duet Accompaniment (Play solo part 1 octave higher than written.)

The Polar Express

Music by Alan Silvestri
Lyrics by Glen Ballard

Arr. by Tom Gerou

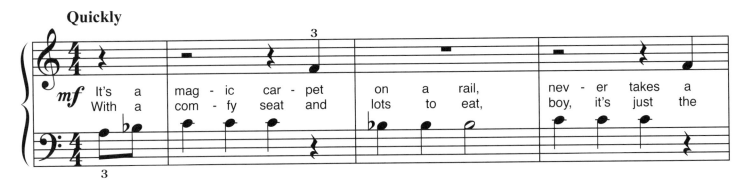

Optional Duet Accompaniment (Play solo part 1 octave higher than written.)

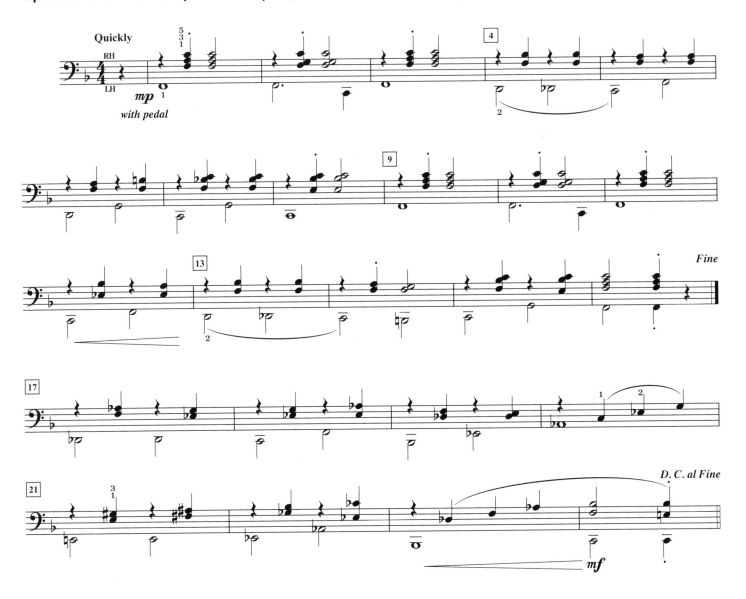

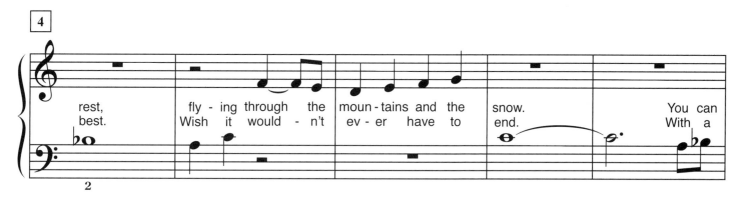

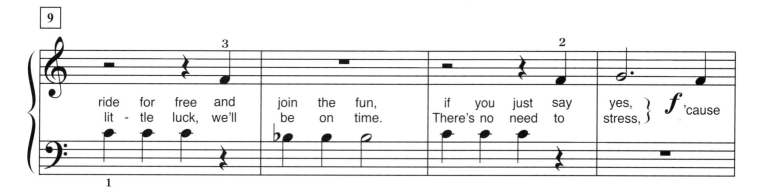

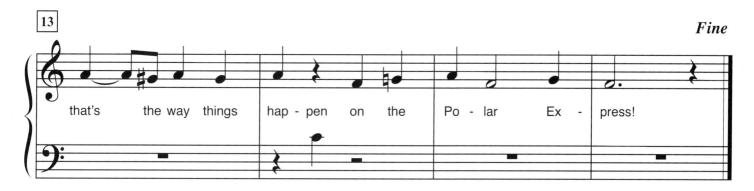

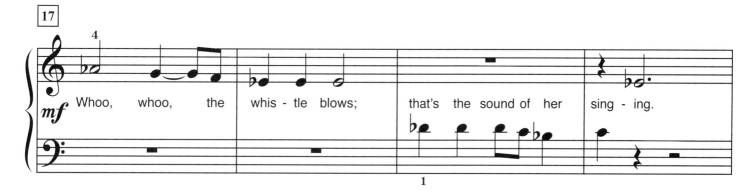

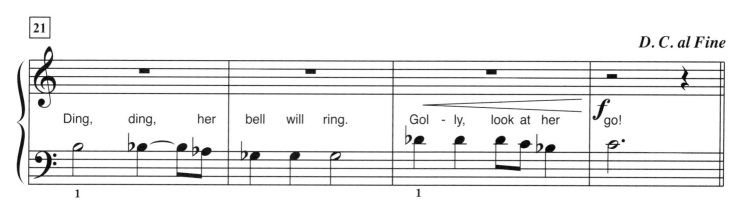

Rockin' Around the Christmas Tree

Words and Music by Johnny Marks

Arr. by Tom Gerou

Moderate swing tempo

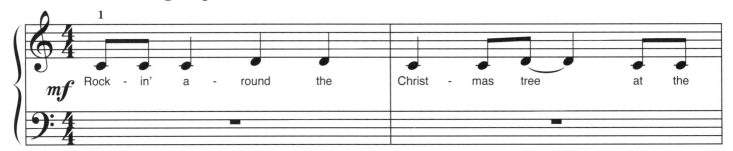

Rock - in' a - round the   Christ - mas tree   at the

Optional Duet Accompaniment (Play solo part 1 octave higher than written.)

Moderate swing tempo

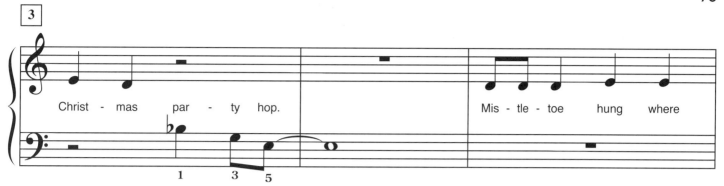

Christ - mas par - ty hop. Mis - tle - toe hung where

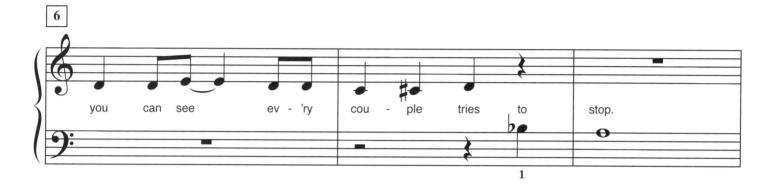

you can see ev - 'ry cou - ple tries to stop.

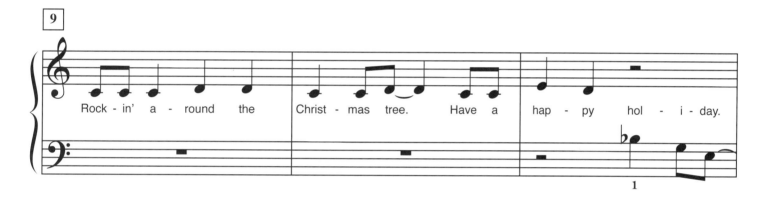

Rock - in' a - round the Christ - mas tree. Have a hap - py hol - i - day.

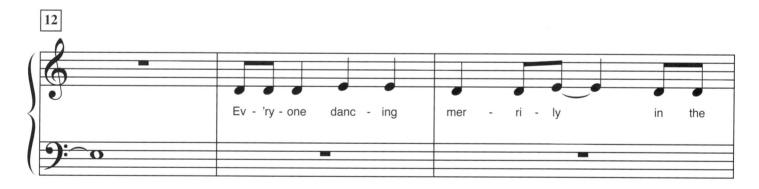

Ev - 'ry - one danc - ing mer - ri - ly in the

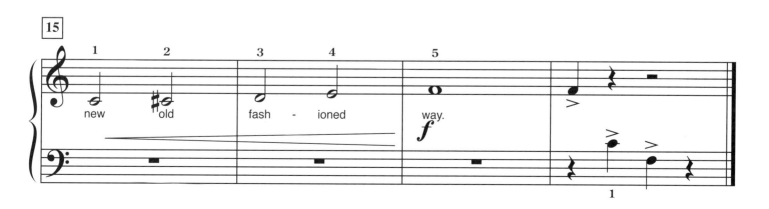

new old fash - ioned way.

Rudolph the Red-Nosed Reindeer

Words and Music by Johnny Marks
Arr. by Tom Gerou

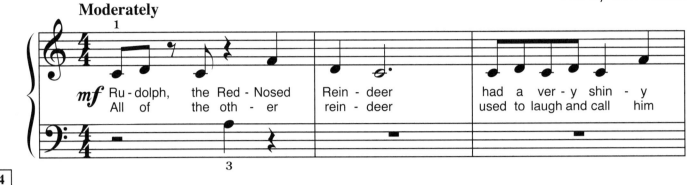

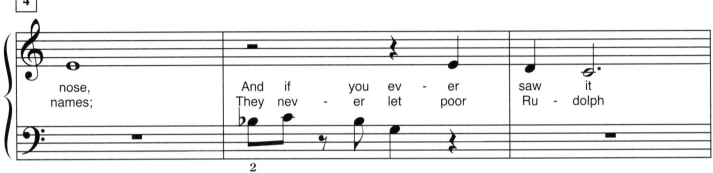

Optional Duet Accompaniment (Play solo part 1 octave higher than written.)

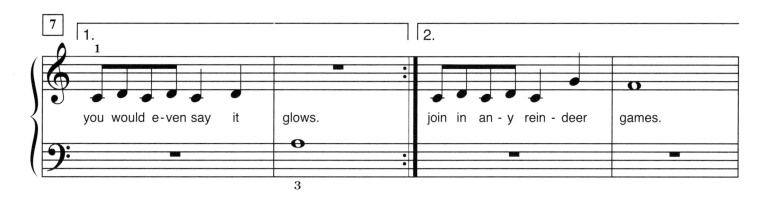

you would e-ven say it glows.

join in an-y rein-deer games.

mp Then one fog-gy Christ-mas Eve, San-ta came to say: "Ru-dolph, with your *mf*

nose so bright, won't you guide my sleigh to-night?" Then how the rein-deer

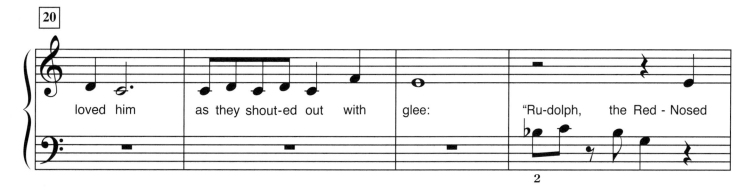

loved him as they shout-ed out with glee: "Ru-dolph, the Red-Nosed

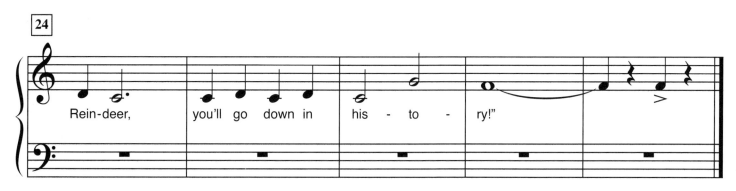

Rein-deer, you'll go down in his - to - ry!"

Russian Dance
(from *The Nutcracker*)

Peter Ilyich Tchaikovsky

Arr. by Tom Gerou

Optional Duet Accompaniment (Play solo part 1 octave higher than written.)

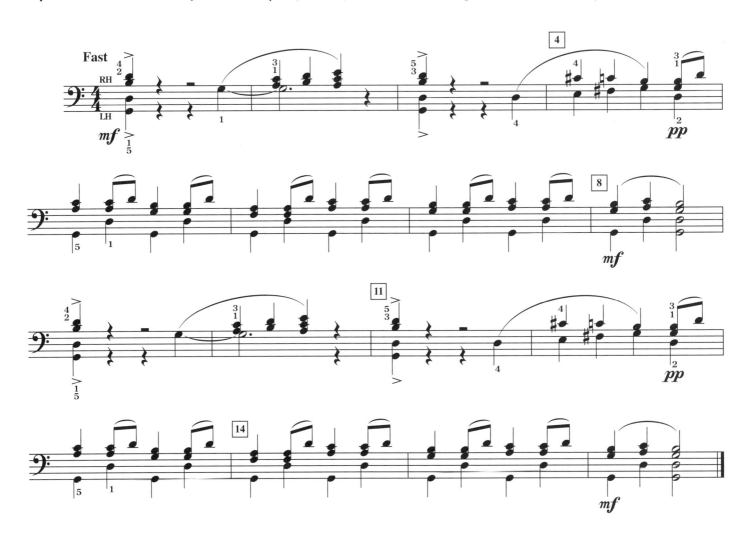

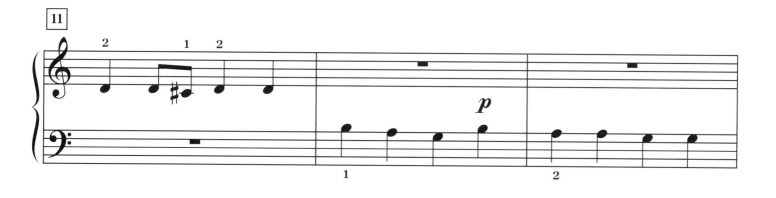

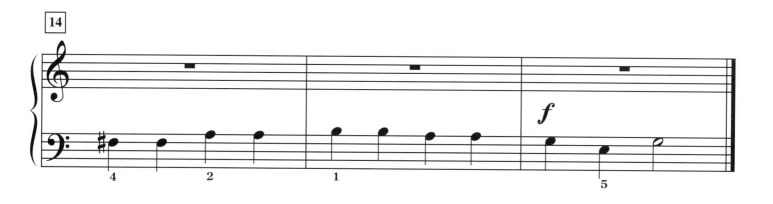

Santa Claus Is Comin' to Town

Music by J. Fred Coots
Words by Haven Gillespie

Arr. by Tom Gerou

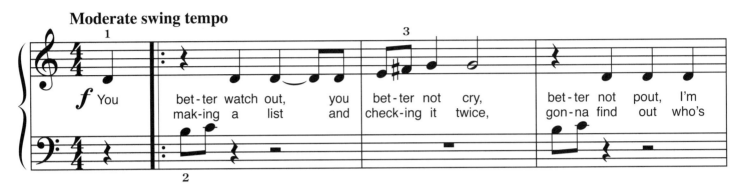

Optional Duet Accompaniment (Play solo part 1 octave higher than written.)

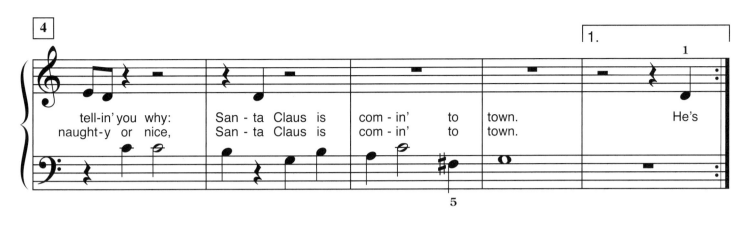

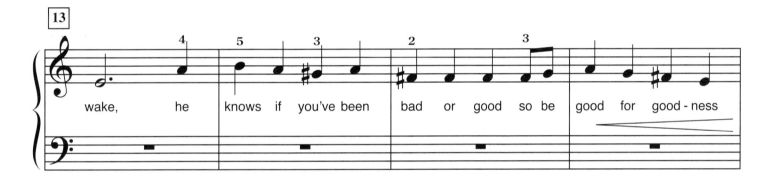

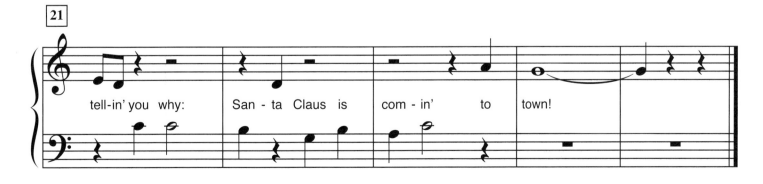

Silent Night

Words by Joseph Mohr
Music by Franz Grüber

Arr. by Tom Gerou

Optional Duet Accompaniment (Play solo part 1 octave higher than written.)

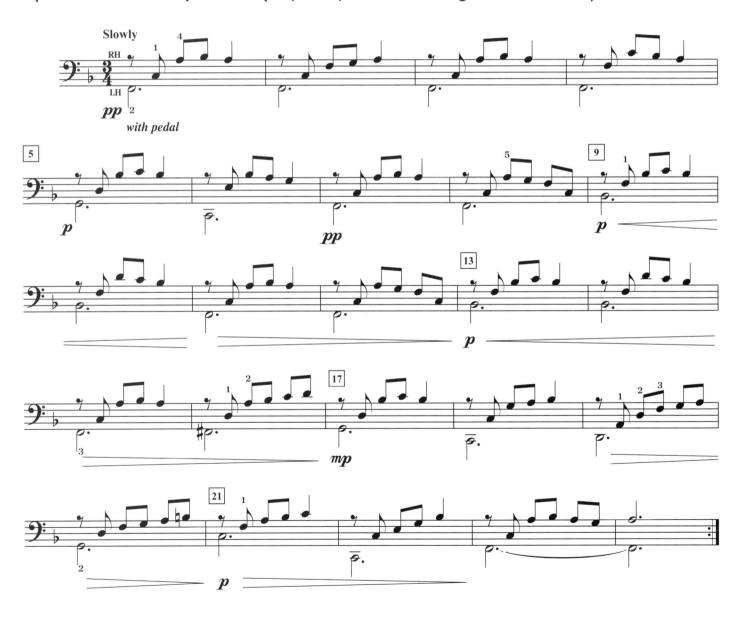

5

9

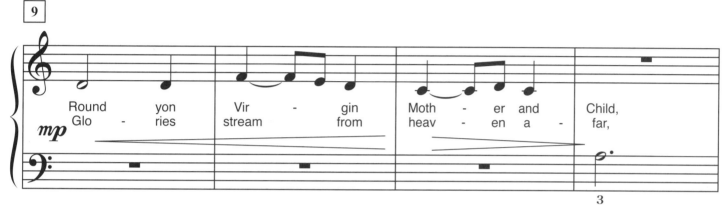

13

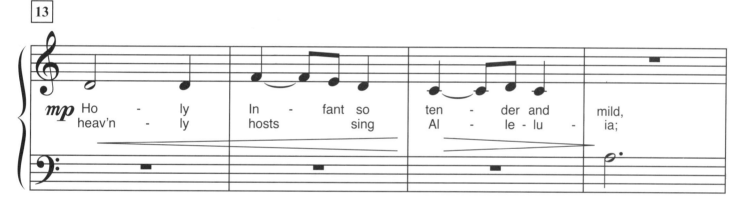

17

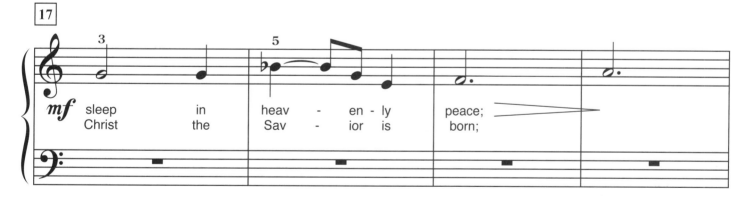

21

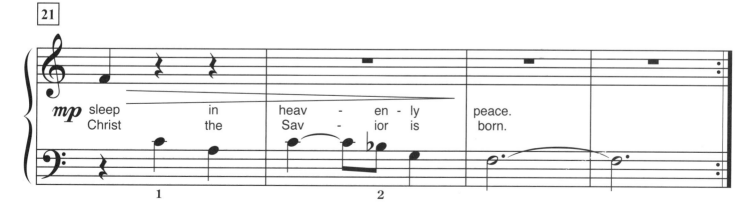

Sleigh Ride

Music by Leroy Anderson
Words by Mitchell Parish

Arr. by Tom Gerou

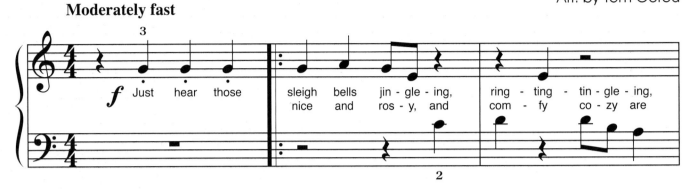

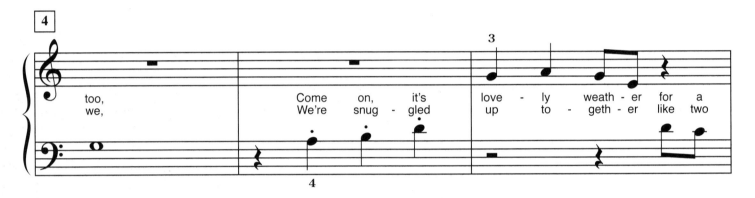

Optional Duet Accompaniment (Play solo part 1 octave higher than written.)

85

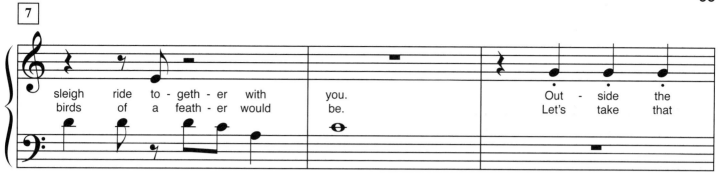

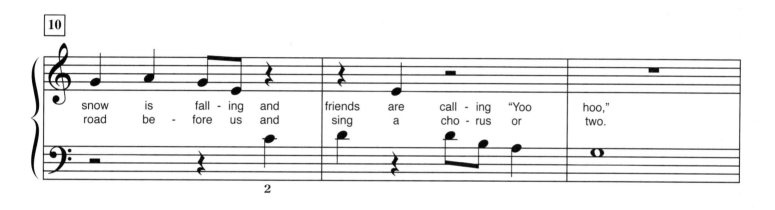

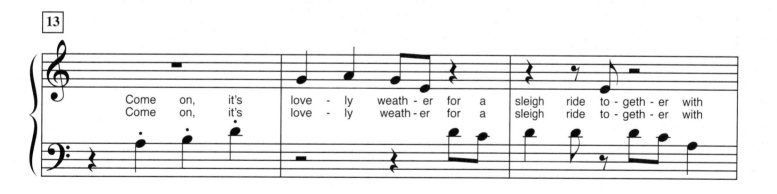

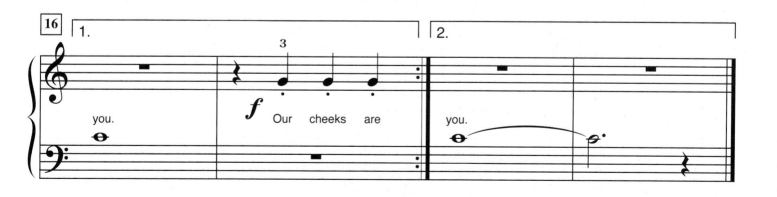

Spirit of the Season
(from *The Polar Express*)

Words and Music by
Glen Ballard and Alan Silvestri
Arr. by Tom Gerou

It's the spir-it of the sea-son. You can feel it in the air.

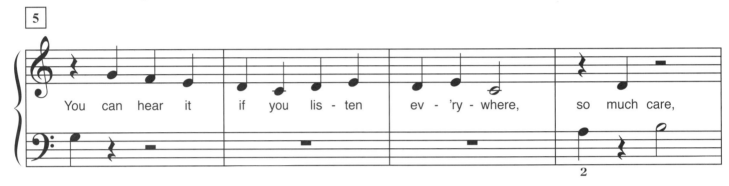

You can hear it if you lis-ten ev-'ry-where, so much care,

Optional Duet Accompaniment (Play solo part 1 octave higher than written.)

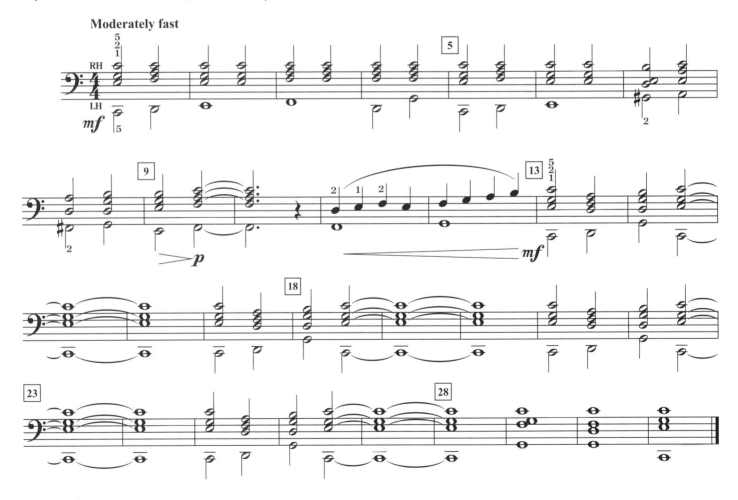

like   a   prayer...   What - ever   it   is,   you   need   to   share   it.

It's   the   spir - it   of   the   sea - son.   You   can   hear   it

in   the   air.   It's   the   spir - it   of   the   sea-son.

You   can   hear   it   ev - 'ry - where.

Toyland
(from *Babes in Toyland*)

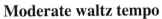

Words by Glen MacDonough
Music by Victor Herbert
Arr. Tom Gerou

Moderate waltz tempo

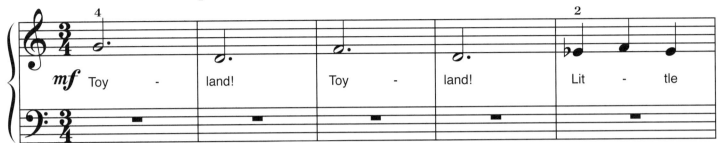

mf Toy - land! Toy - land! Lit - tle

Optional Duet Accompaniment (Play solo part 1 octave higher than written.)

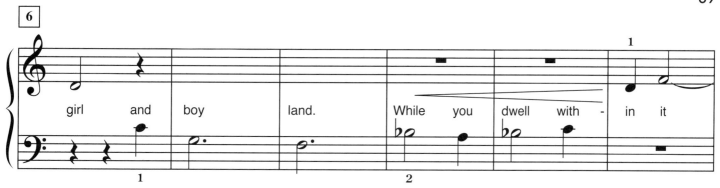

girl and boy land. While you dwell with - in it

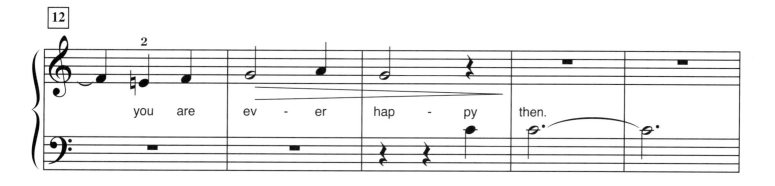

you are ev - er hap - py then.

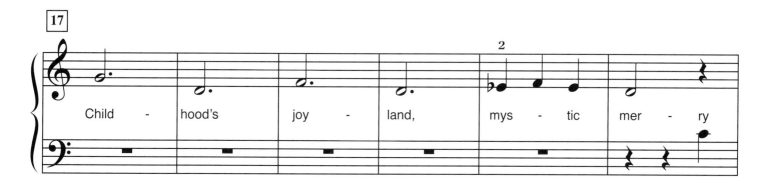

Child - hood's joy - land, mys - tic mer - ry

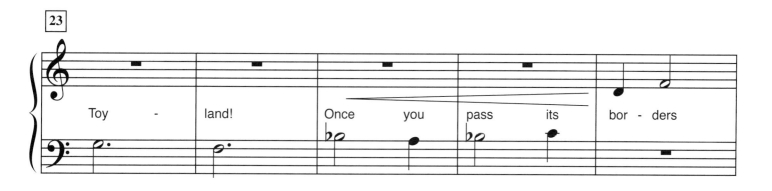

Toy - land! Once you pass its bor - ders

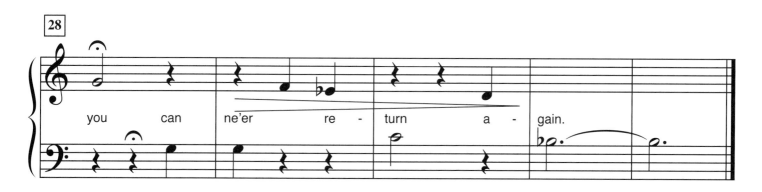

you can ne'er re - turn a - gain.

Up on the Housetop

Words and Music by Benjamin Hanby
Arr. by Tom Gerou

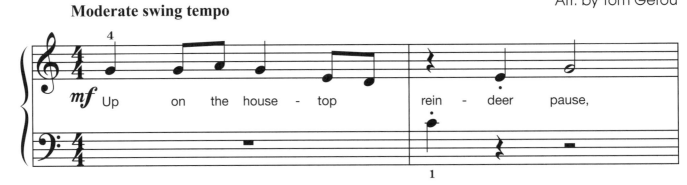

Optional Duet Accompaniment (Play solo part 1 octave higher than written.)

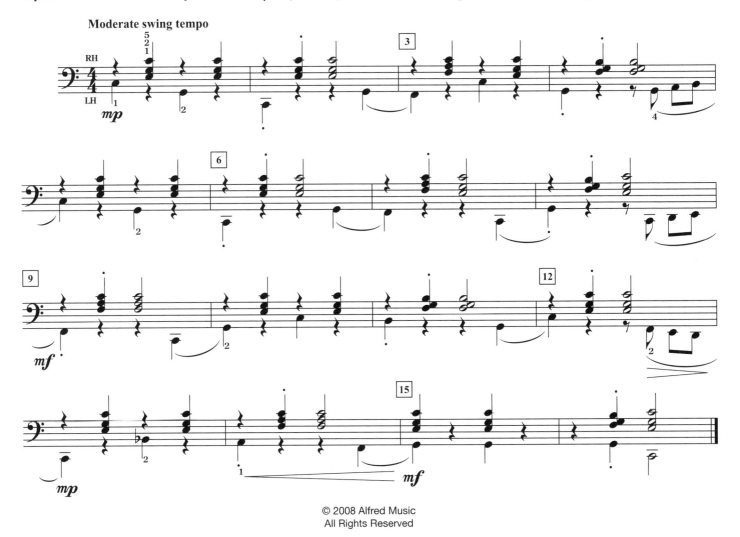

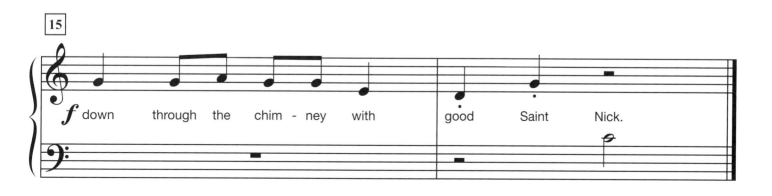

Waltz of the Flowers
(from *The Nutcracker*)

Peter Ilyich Tchaikovsky
Arr. by Tom Gerou

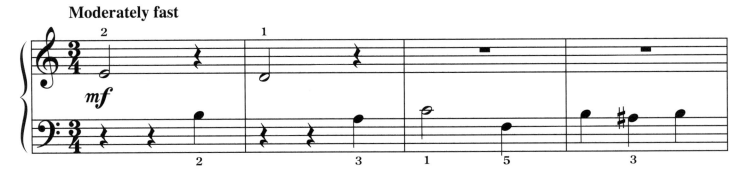

Optional Duet Accompaniment (Play solo part 1 octave higher than written.)

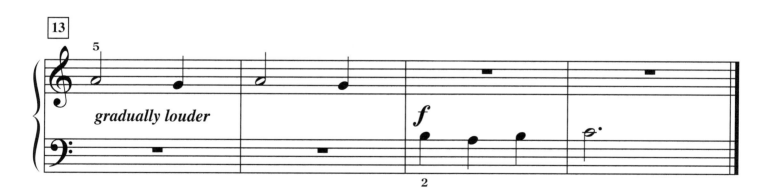

We Three Kings

John Henry Hopkins, Jr.

Arr. by Tom Gerou

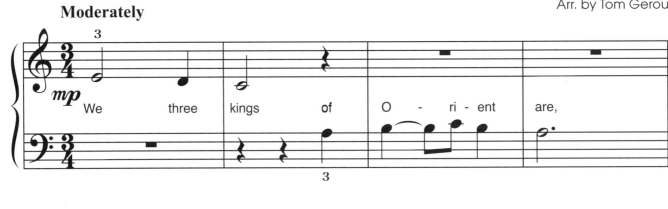

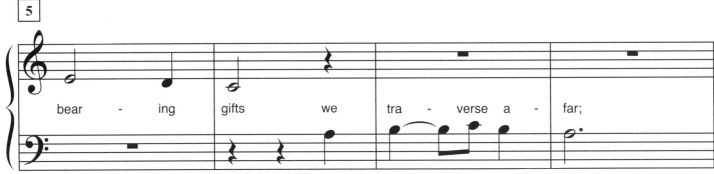

Optional Duet Accompaniment (Play solo part 1 octave higher than written.)

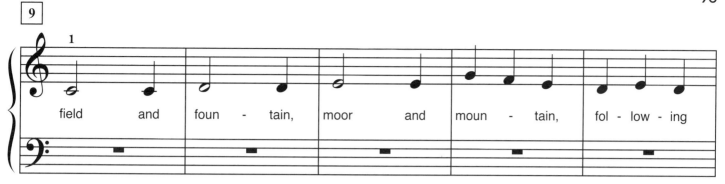

9

field and foun - tain, moor and moun - tain, fol - low - ing

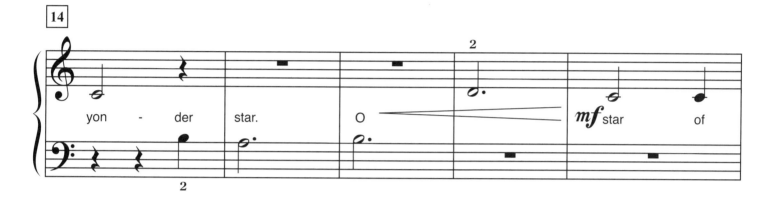

14

yon - der star. O *mf* star of

19

won - der, star of night, star with roy - al

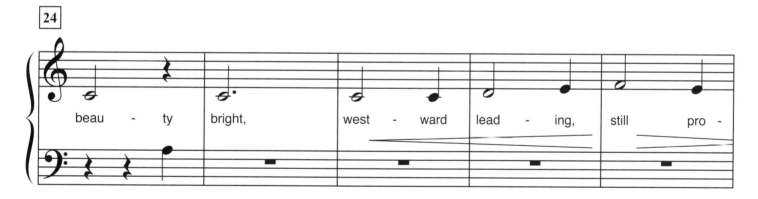

24

beau - ty bright, west - ward lead - ing, still pro -

29

ceed - ing, *mp* guide us to Thy per - fect light.

We Wish You a Merry Christmas

Traditional English Carol
Arr. by Tom Gerou

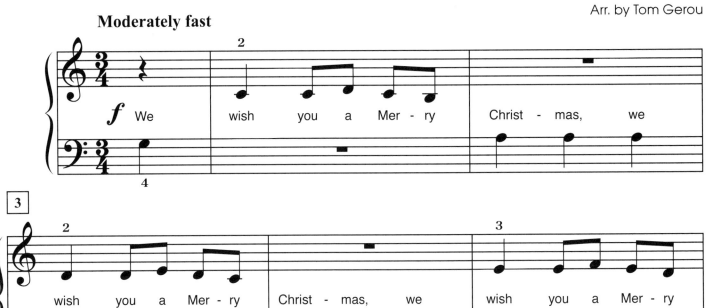

Optional Duet Accompaniment (Play solo part 1 octave higher than written.)

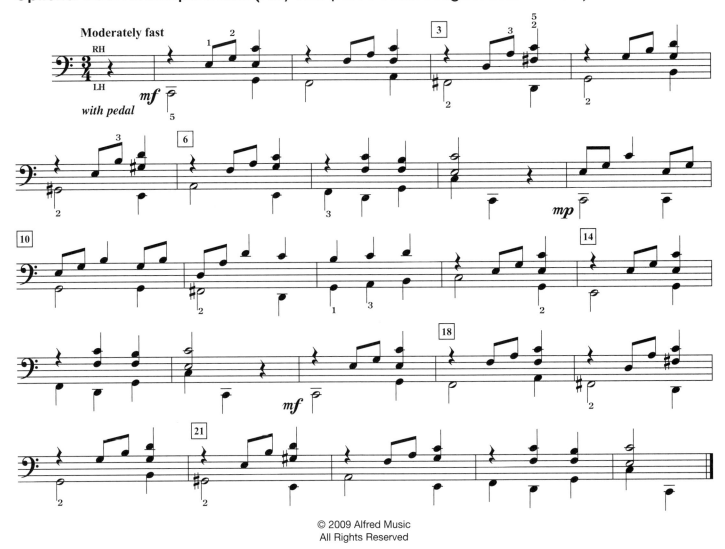

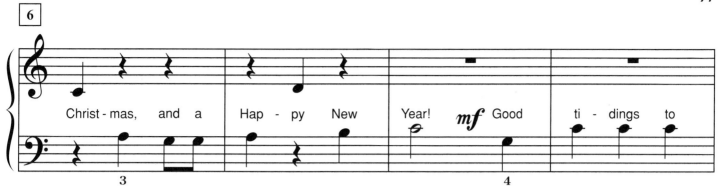

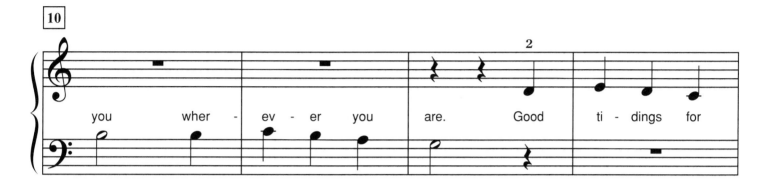

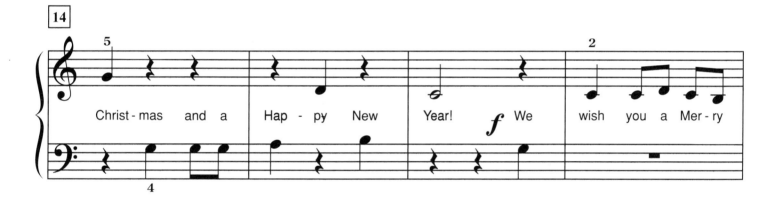

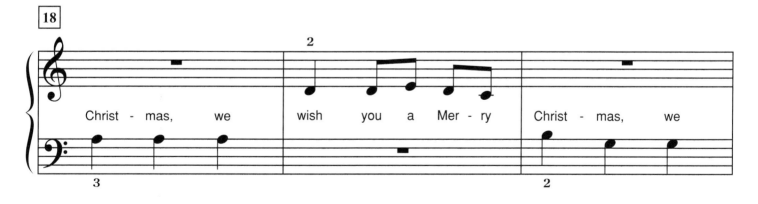

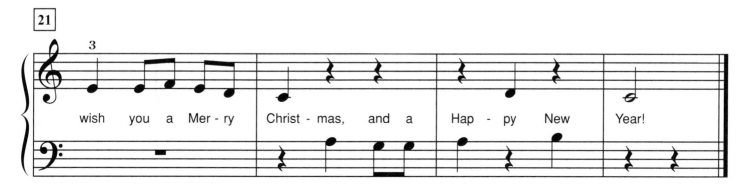

When Christmas Comes to Town
(from *The Polar Express*)

Music by Alan Silvestri
Lyrics by Glen Ballard
Arr. by Tom Gerou

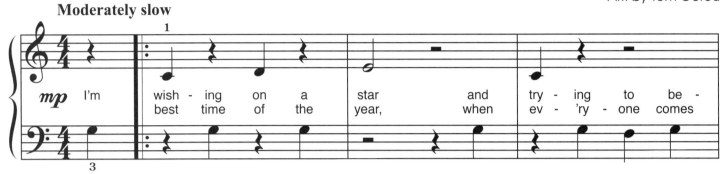

Optional Duet Accompaniment (Play solo part 1 octave higher than written.)

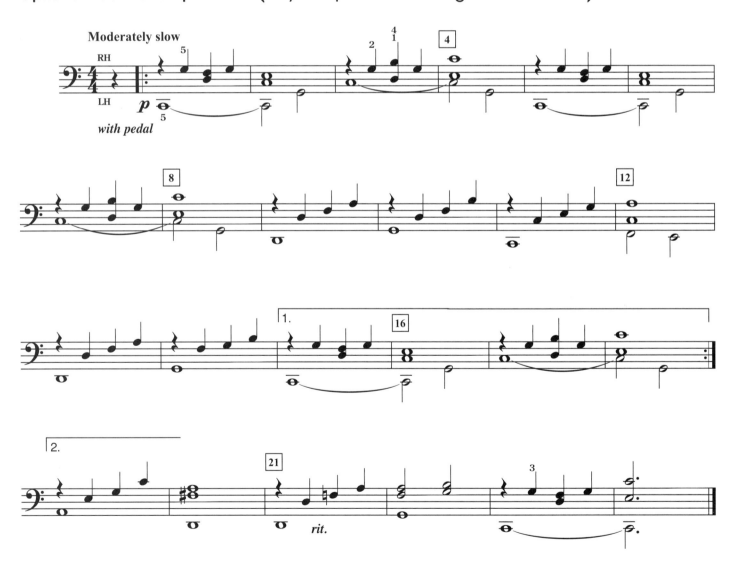

lieve that, e - ven though it's far, he'll find me Christ - mas
home; with all this Christ - mas cheer it's hard to be a -

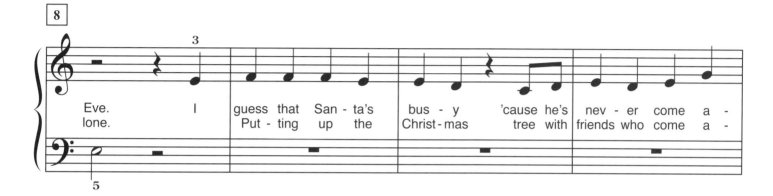

Eve. I guess that San - ta's bus - y 'cause he's nev - er come a -
lone. Put - ting up the Christ - mas tree with friends who come a -

round. I think of him when Christ - mas comes to town.
round, it's so much fun when Christ - mas comes to

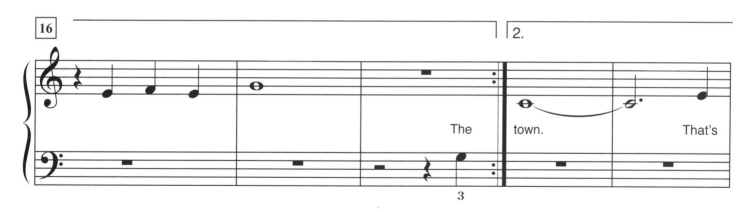

The town. That's

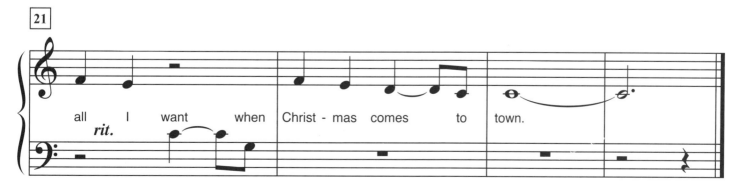

all I want when Christ - mas comes to town.

rit.

Winter Wonderland

Words by Dick Smith
Music by Felix Bernard

Arr. by Tom Gerou

Optional Duet Accompaniment (Play solo part 1 octave higher than written.)

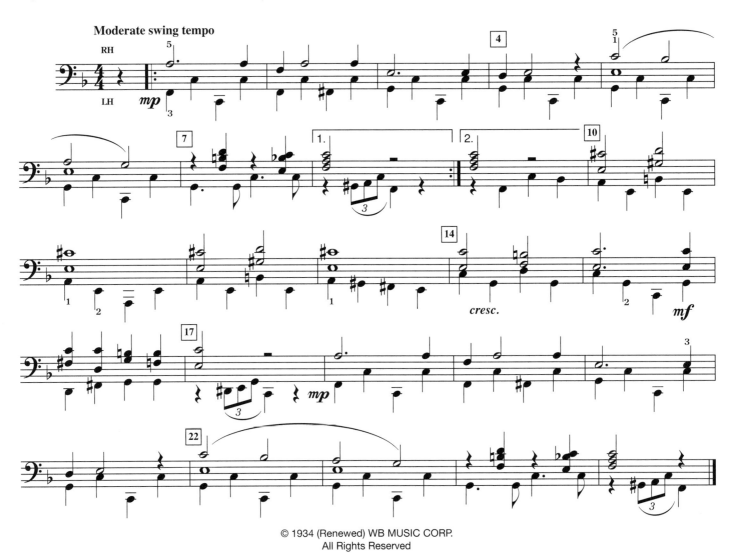

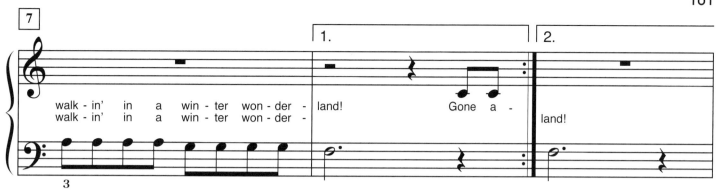

walk - in' in a win - ter won - der - land! Gone a -
walk - in' in a win - ter won - der - land!

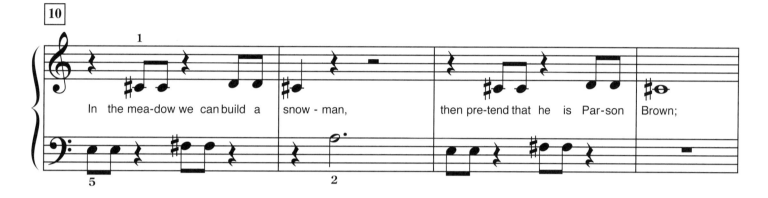

In the mea-dow we can build a snow - man, then pre-tend that he is Par-son Brown;

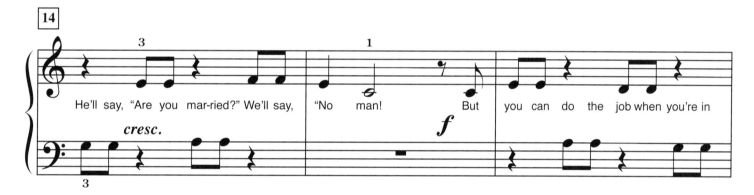

He'll say, "Are you mar-ried?" We'll say, "No man! But you can do the job when you're in

cresc. *f*

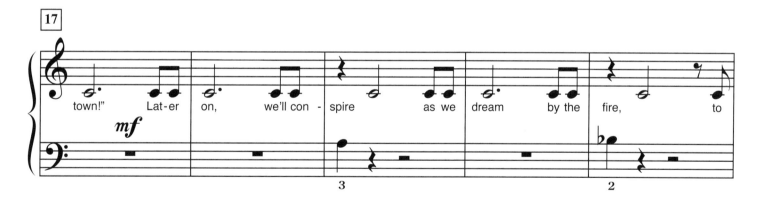

town!" Lat-er on, we'll con - spire as we dream by the fire, to

mf

face un - a-fraid the plans that we made, walk-in' in a win-ter won-der - land!

'Zat You, Santa Claus?

Words and Music by Jack Fox
Arr. by Tom Gerou

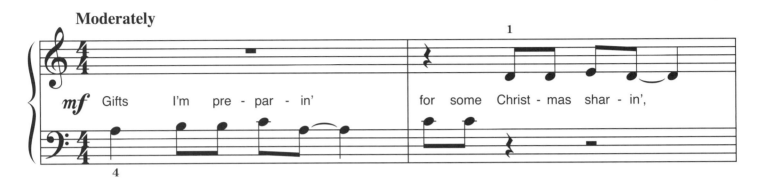

Optional Duet Accompaniment (Play solo part 1 octave higher than written.)

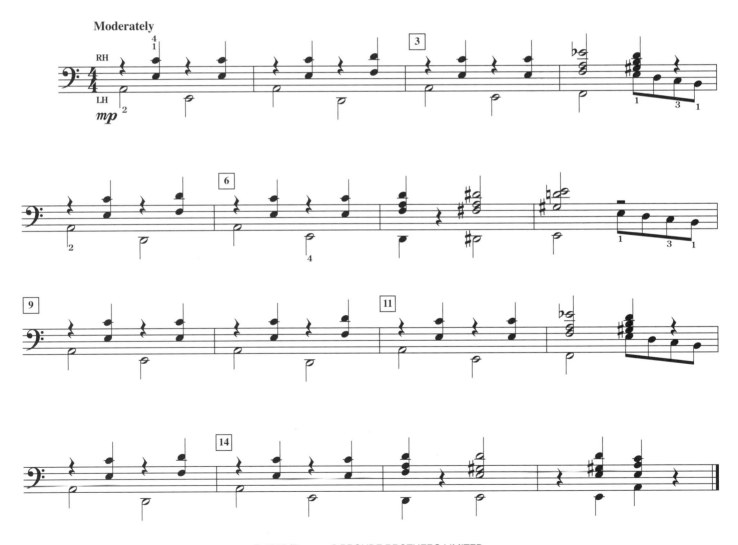

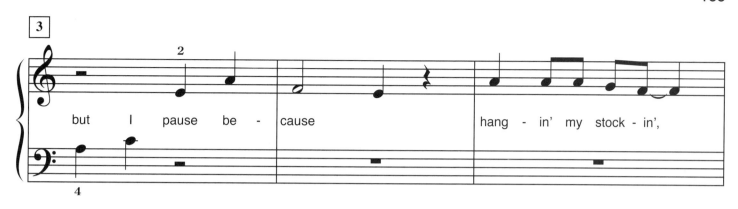

but I pause be - cause   hang - in' my stock - in',

I can hear a knock - in'.   'Zat you, San - ta   Claus?

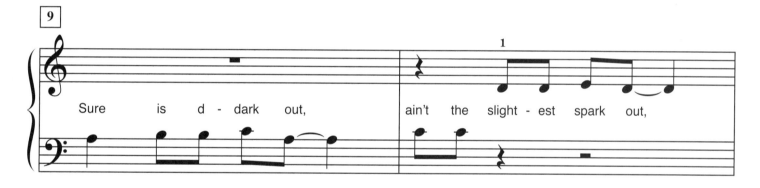

Sure is d - dark out,   ain't the slight - est spark out,

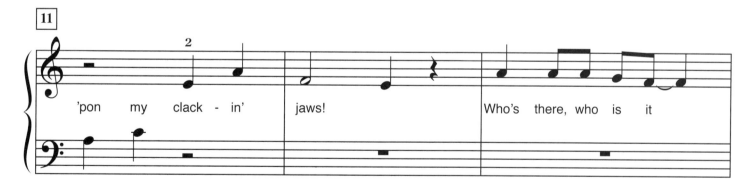

'pon my clack - in'   jaws!   Who's there, who is it

stop - pin' for a vis - it?   'Zat you, San - ta   Claus?